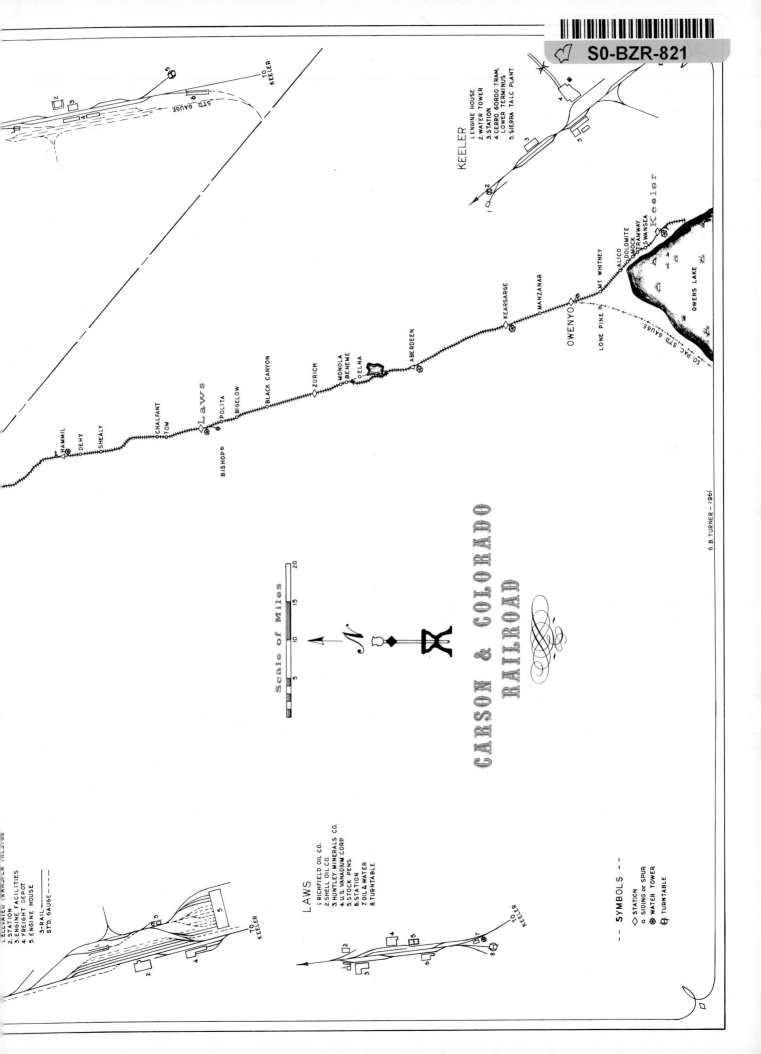

KEELER
1. ENGINE HOUSE
2. WATER TOWER
3. STATION
4. CERRO GORDO TRAM, LOWER TERMINUS
5. SIERRA TALC PLANT

Keeler

ALICO
DOLOMITE
MOCK
TRAMWAY
SWANSEA

OWENS LAKE

MT. WHITNEY

OWENYO

LONE PINE

SO. PAC. STD. GAUGE

MANZANAR

KEARSARGE

ABERDEEN

OELNA
BENEME
MONOLA

ZURICH

BLACK CANYON

BIGELOW
POLITA

Laws

BISHOP

TOM
CHALFANT

SHEALY
DEHY
HAMMIL

TO KEELER

STD. GAUGE

CARSON & COLORADO
RAILROAD

Scale of Miles
5   10   15   20

N

G. B. TURNER – 1961

3-RAIL
STD. GAUGE ------

1. ELEVATED _____
2. STATION
3. ENGINE FACILITIES
4. FREIGHT DEPOT
5. ENGINE HOUSE

LAWS
1. RICHFIELD OIL CO.
2. SHELL OIL CO.
3. HUNTLEY MINERALS CO.
4. U.S. VANADIUM CORP.
5. STOCK PENS
6. STATION
7. OIL & WATER
8. TURNTABLE

TO KEELER

TO KEELER

~ ~ SYMBOLS ~ ~
◇ STATION
○ SIDING or SPUR
✳ WATER TOWER
⊖ TURNTABLE

SLIM RAILS THROUGH THE SAND

. . . the Railroad that "began nowhar, ended nowhar, an' stopped all night to think it over . . ."

Jim Butler
Tonopah, Nevada

*C&C Engine No. 5, her brass polished and "freshly wooded up,"
provides a symbolic scene with her crew beside the Candelaria,
Nevada station.*

*. . . Right:
Kearsarge water tank,
basking in the sun of the
Owens Valley.*

*Dust Jacket
Cover Photo by Fred Hust*

SLIM RAILS THROUGH THE SAND

THE SAND

by George Turner

The Saga of the Carson & Colorado-Southern Pacific Narrow-Gauge Railroad through the Desert

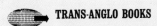

TRANS-ANGLO BOOKS

DONALD DUKE COLLECTION

ACKNOWLEDGEMENTS

As with most historical publications, this book would not have seen print without the gracious help of many persons. My profound appreciation goes to Art Haig, Dick Datin and Walt Stampfli for their generous efforts during the gathering of material. In addition, my thanks go also to the Eastern California Museum and the Bancroft Library for their kind cooperation.

It is obvious that many painstaking hours are required to produce a scale prototype drawing. Al Barker, Herb Cearley and Dick Tucker considerably eased this task, as can be seen in their excellent contributions.

To Lottie Arcularius, Gerald Best, Don Duke, Fred Hust, Hugh Tolford and all others whose names appear in the photo credits, the author is indeed grateful.

One final and important facet is the job of transforming the assembled material into the final format. Words cannot express my gratitude to Hank Johnston for his continuing assistance throughout this effort.

SLIM RAILS THROUGH THE SAND
The Saga of the Carson & Colorado-Southern Pacific Narrow-Gauge Railroad through the Desert

By GEORGE TURNER

ISBN: 0-87046-016-1

Library of Congress Catalog Card No: 68:24093

THIRD EDITION (REVISED)

FOURTH PRINTING, APRIL 1974

Printed and Bound in The United States of America

Published by Trans-Anglo Books
P.O. Box 38 • Corona Del Mar, California 92625

Issued by

Bishop Museum & Historical Society

Good for: One Climb on Locomotive No. 9
Ring the Bell!
Laws Railroad Museum & Historical Site.

The Person Accepting This

FREE TICKET

AGREES to conform to all Rules and Regulations set forth by the County of Inyo and the Bishop Museum and Historical Society.

Visiting Hours: 10:00 A.M. - 4:00 P. M. Daily

Date: MAR 12 1979

CHALFANT PRESS, BISHOP, CA.

DONALD DUKE COLLECTION

Owens Valley "Daylight Special"

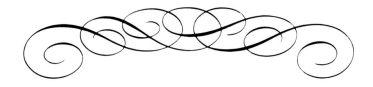

Foreword

During the latter portion of the nineteenth century the colorful narrow gauge railroads comprised a good percentage of the country's total trackage. Diminutive engines and cars rattled their way along every type of terrain imaginable. Speed records and comfort were left to the big roads . . . sheer adventure at no extra cost was normally available on the narrow gauge.

In contrast with cross country lines, the slim rails were usually born of local necessities . . . mining, logging, livestock, etc. The very nature of these industries was to ultimately cause the roads' demise. Local conditions either outgrew the 3 foot facilities or faded entirely from any need of narrow gauge rail service. Some of today's large cities began as railposts in a wilderness along a transcontinental line. In comparison, most of the prominent narrow gauge points are now unheard of.

Mountain regions were usually better suited to narrow gauge applications as opposed to standard gauge. The smaller and lighter engines could negotiate tighter curves. Rolling stock, rail and related equipment were more economical and required less space . . . in some areas, this was very critical. It is indeed a real thrill to peer out of a coach window on an outside curve in the Rockies and see no visible means of support!

The last two common-carrier narrow gauge roads that survived into modern times were of somewhat different entities. Famed for its locale high in the Rockies, the Denver & Rio Grande was reasonably well equipped. Engine facilities were numerous, compared with other light iron roads of the period. Scenery along the right of way was, for the most part, spectacular. Every apparent requisite for survival existed. Today, the Silverton Branch enjoys ever increasing passenger revenue from its remaining trackage . . . her Mikados steaming through the canyon and around the cliffs, oblivious of the missile age.

Way out West, the other road (now dismantled) boasted precious little in the way of new equipment. After 1885, all of its motive power and rolling stock were of "hand-me-down" variety. The line was never completed and realized only half of its intended trackage. Attractions along the line included glaring sand, barren hills, intense heat and jack-rabbits. One scenic treat did exist for the intrepid traveler to the end of the line . . . the mighty Sierras and Mt. Whitney. Such was the Carson & Colorado. It is with reference to those slim rails through the sand that the contents are dedicated.

For those who have an additional interest in model railroading, a portion is presented. Prototype plans may vary from what the final pieces of rolling stock appeared to be. Engines and cars were altered as the immediate situation required. During such occasions, replacement parts or conversions were generally taken from the storage track. Flat cars provided the basic structure for many variations of the freight roster. Some pieces first saw service on the Florence & Cripple Creek, were sent to the South Pacific Coast and then to the Keeler Branch, victims of continual abandonment.

Electronic signals now beam from giant reflectors where once the casual sound of the narrow gauge whistle blew. May this book provide some nostalgia of an era passed.

George Turner

Dick Datin

Narrow Gauge In A Wilderness

As each period of our history passes, circumstances have managed to provide trends for consuming the time of enterprising tycoons. Before the turn of the century, the ability of one to promote a rail venture was a definite status symbol. At a time when fortunes were being made in the western mining camps, those who were able to parlay this wealth into the Iron Horse could vision no end to prosperity.

Out in Nevada, the fabulous Comstock Lode was represented by the Virginia & Truckee, founded in 1868, linking Virginia City to Reno and the Central Pacific R.R. The post-civil war years saw other proposals for trackage in the area being germinated in many a pine-panelled office. One example was the charter granted to the Esmeralda & Walker River R.R. in 1864. This was to be a route to Aurora, an up and coming boom town. A later, similar venture was a plan by the Western Nevada R.R. Co. in early 1880 for a road to Candelaria.

In those days, a fully equipped railroad could be ordered largely from builders' catalogs . . . which no doubt fueled the flame of many of these proposals. With very few exceptions the only track set down by these proposals were rail samples used for paperweights.

Getting down to reality, it took the astute promotion of William Sharon, know-how of Hume Yerington and the well-heeled assistance of Darius Mills to get things moving. One cannot overlook the logic here, as these same men controlled the V&T. The Carson Times of April 18, 1880 reported that the "Bodie Extension" was going to materialize, according to "sources believed to be thoroughly reliable." Twenty-two days later on May 10, the Carson & Colorado Railroad Co. was incorporated.

The route and destination of the newly formed C&C was hardly more than conjecture even as the first spikes were being driven at Mound House. It was generally accepted that the roads' title implied that it would connect the rivers of the same names, some 600 miles in all. Surveys to both Bodie and Candelaria had been made, but beyond this, it was anyone's guess as to where the rail might go.

Three foot gauge was established for the road as a matter of simple economics. There were to be no requirements for lavish Pullmans, posh coaches or other frills. After all, passenger service in a combine would surpass the stage. Remember also, most of the customers were gun-toting hombres on their way to roaring mining towns . . . and this could prove detrimental to costly varnish being 'altered' by stray bullets and carefree cowboys. During negotiations for the initial right of way, a portion of the line traversed the Schurz Indian reservation. This resulted in an agreement to haul our original Americans for free. Like many of the early "benefits" bestowed upon the Red Man, this gratis transportation was furnished in the form of full view accommodations atop the coach or box car roofs.

Actual construction of the railroad got off to a very slow start. Six months after incorporation only three miles of track had been put down . . . in ten months the line had progressed only 70 miles. The terrain posed no problem, as the right of way was routed over the most open coun-

Beginning of "nowhar;" the site of Mound House, Nevada.

try imaginable. Initial delays arose over the use of Chinese labor. The Comstock Lode was in a slump which provided a surplus of men. The going rate for Chinese help was a dollar a day for a 26 day month (less $15 a month for provisions.) This left little for life's essentials such as gambling, booze, women, etc., and left even less incentive for the available ex-miners. Added to the labor quarrels, materials were slow in arriving. Rails were imported from Europe to save costs and in 1880 it was a real feat to get ocean shipments within 3 to 6 months of promised delivery. The railroad was virtually waiting for its ship to come in!

A point at the south end of Walker Lake was established as the first "terminus" . . . a tent city called Hawthorne. This location would serve the purpose for later decisions as to continuing either to Bodie or to Candelaria or both. To this end the Chinese workers were put, removing them as a source for squabbles at the Mound House section. The first train into Hawthorne arrived in the late Spring of 1881. It was of the excursion variety and was sponsored by the

C&C to promote the sale of the local sandy real estate. This was quite natural, as the C&C brass owned the land! Today, Hawthorne remains as the largest city to have been located on the original route, whereas the large existing boom towns of the 80's have all but vanished.

During the summer of 1881 the decision was made to start construction of the road to Candelaria, Nevada. The adopted route required the building of two trestles on the approaches to the town. One structure was 200 feet in length and the other slightly shorter. In March of 1882, the railroad and also a water pipe line, both being well received, reached into Candelaria. From here the announced objective of the C&C was to push on to Mojave, California, passing through the Owens Valley. The roadbed was to eventually go through Montgomery Pass at an elevation of over 7100 feet . . . this was higher than the Southern Pacific crossing of Donner Summit. Descent into Owens Valley was made at times on gradients of 3.2 per cent and included a tunnel hewed from solid rock, 247 feet long.

News of the pending arrival of rail service into the Owens Valley was naturally eagerly anticipated by the residents. Several towns were well established and one can easily imagine their disgust to learn that the C&C iron would by-pass them all. Consequently the arrival of the narrow gauge was hardly mentioned as it wended its way down the eastern portion of the valley floor towards Keeler, at the end of Owens Lake. Keeler was already located on the proposed route, due mainly to the expected revenue from the activity at the lofty Cerro Gordo mines.

1882 saw 200 miles of rail in operation from Mound House, Nevada, to Benton, California. From a gross revenue of $442,254 a tidy 25 per cent profit was realized during the first full year of business. By August of 1883 the rails had gone down to Keeler . . . and so did the profits, to the consternation of the management. With this turn of events, the subject of any further trackage was avoided by the front office. There were many rumors in the next few years of future expansion, but these never materialized.

Many attempts were naturally made to offset the continuing loss of revenue. Assistant Superintendent Laws imposed a salary reduction upon

Decked out in the "uniform of the day," Fred Balzar typified the early day conductor. Mr. Balzar went on to greater things, becoming the Governor of Nevada in 1932.

Engine No. 3, the Colorado, awaits word as to departure time . . .

himself as one of the many means to improve the black side of the ledger. Productivity of the mining areas along the route was the key to the economic success of the railroad and by 1886, most of them had passed their peak. Occasional flurries of activity would flare up, but these were of short duration and the profit picture remained dim for the road. This condition resulted in a shuffling of the C&C deck in 1892, incorporating the "Railroad" into a "Railway." In effect, this was largely a 'paper' maneuver to reduce the accumulated debt, with no change in actual ownership. There were no operating losses as a result of the revised bookwork but the earnings for the next eight years were not enough to cover even a nominal interest for the investors. As 1899 came to a close, Sharon had passed away, Mills was in the East and Yerington had other more pressing interests that diverted his attention from the desert "loss leader."

After twenty years of experiencing everything but a favorable bank balance, the C&C officials were quite naturally ripe for a sale. It would be an understatement to say that they were "receptive" to the Southern Pacific offer in March of 1900 to the tune of $2,750,000. The subject of a possible sale of the neighboring Virginia & Truckee was also kicked around, but an agreeable price tag wasn't negotiated. The V&T wasn't faring much better than the Carson & Colorado at the turn of the century but it was felt that conditions affecting the standard gauge line would improve.

No sooner had the S.P. check passed the clearing house, than Fate was at work on a surprise for the new owners that probably turned Sharon over in his grave. Two months after the sale of the C&C, an itinerate prospector, Jim Butler, tripped over a silver outcropping in the San Antonio mountains while looking for his pack mule. The rest is history . . . Tonopah was born. Needless to say, this turn of events and the subsequent gold discoveries at Goldfield in 1904 woke up the "Sleeping Princess." Unheard of traffic tie-ups began occurring at Mound House. Perishable goods were given top priority, of course. It didn't take long, however, for the fast-buck artists to label their gambling machinery "perishable"!

In a short period of time the S.P. realized the return of its original investment. It wasn't too much later that it became apparent that the dual gauge condition at Mound House needed a remedy for the continual delays. At the time of transfer of the C&C to the Southern Pacific, it was generally assumed that the line would be standard gauged. Obviously the prime reason for S.P. acquisition was for a connecting route from

Link and pin couplers date this photo, taken at Wabuska, to C&C days prior to 1897.

Engine No. 17 makes a brief inspection stop near Queen in 1907.

Mt. Montgomery Pass in 1905. The team shown was used in road construction making way for the automobile (paving came much later!). Note the interchange of Tonopah Railroad narrow gauge cars.

Ogden to Los Angeles . . . C&C profits could hardly be a consideration. So it came as no surprise when the cut-off connection from Churchill to Hazen was built in 1905, along with the broad gauging from Mound House to Mina. Hereafter, the only growth on the V&T was the weeds along its right of way.

Between 1900 and 1905, the Southern Pacific retained the Carson & Colorado Railway as a wholly-owned subsidiary. A new corporate structure was chartered in 1905 as the Nevada & California Railroad Company, also wholly owned by the S.P. With the construction of the Los Angeles aqueduct, demands for rail transportation increased and the long awaited rail connection to Mojave was started in 1908. The 144 mile "Jawbone Branch" from Mojave to the newly situated Owenyo connection on the N&C was completed in 1911. On the northern end, other activity was in the mill . . . Copper mining had been revived. The sounds of 'let's build a railroad' echoed in the Mason Valley and the Nevada Copper Belt R.R. emerged. This 38 mile short line connected with the N&C at Wabuska, Nevada and was operated by various interests until 1947.

Another paper shuffle was made in 1912 that removed the Nevada & California R.R. from the books. The accounts and property were then transferred to the Central Pacific for administration. Car lettering reflected C.P.-S.P. ownership for the next 48 years of operation. During this time the remaining 150 miles of narrow gauge trackage witnessed two nearby and unique projects get underway, both being located near Keeler.

In 1911, construction was started on a 13½ mile aerial tramway by the Saline Valley Salt Co., for transporting salt from the Saline Valley over the Inyo mountains to the Owens Valley railhead. The terrain was much too rugged for a rail extension other than a very costly circuitous route around the mountains. The first bucket of salt was discharged at the new terminus at "Tramway" on July 2, 1913, but the jubilant operators enjoyed only a brief smell of success. Through an 'oversight,' the original specifications called for capability of handling dry salt. High brine content of the Saline Valley salt created such an overweight condition that the grips on the buckets would not hold on the very steep angles that the cables traversed. By partially filling the buckets, this problem was overcome . . . at the penalty of inefficient delivery rates and increased operating costs. This led to a short lived operation, as revised equipment would be needed, being both extensive and too costly when coupled with the existing expenditures. A portion of the Saline Valley tram can still be seen standing idly by on the eastern slope of

This view looking west from the Saline Valley depicts the construction during 1912 of the tram towers.

LILLIAN HILDERMAN COLLECTION

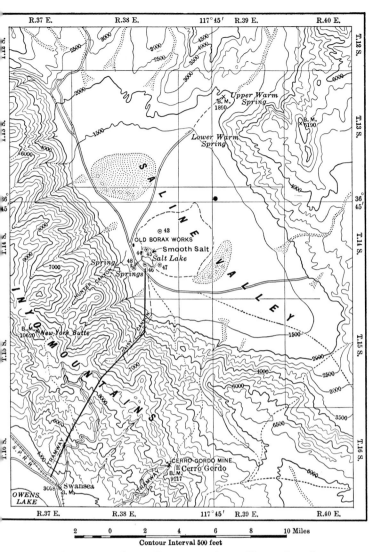

Next came the erection of the Cerro Gordo tramway in 1915. (see page 30) Although long passed its prime, enough zinc and silver remained at the lofty mine to make the tramway a profitable venture for a number of years. Operation of the tram was suspended in 1927 due to a combination of events . . . maintenance on the tram was ever increasing; good ore was thinning out, and the tram operator (and construction foreman for the Saline Valley tram) Mr. Harry Hilderman, passed away. Today, the remnants of the Cerro Gordo tram repose in several heaps near the ghost town of Candelaria, Nevada . . . having been removed from the Owens Valley in 1960 by a mining promoter for an intended venture at the Candelaria site.

Aside from these activities, the 'Slim Princess' was relegated to a very relaxed schedule during her last 30-odd years of operations. As other narrow gauge roads under S.P. jurisdiction underwent either standard gauging or abandonment, most of their equipment found its way to the Mina yards for storage or occasional supplemental use over the desert trackage into the Owens Valley. With the removal of the rails over Mt. Montgomery, the equipment roster shortened accordingly. Agriculture diminished with the transfer of Owens Valley water to Southern California . . . mining towns along the line had long evaporated . . . and little attention was given to the S.P. slim rail feeder as it rattled on through sand and sagebrush to antiquity.

LOCATION OF AERIAL TRAMWAY OF SALINE VALLEY SALT COMPANY

Contour Interval 500 feet

The Saline Valley Salt Mill at Tramway, 1915. Track to the left connected to the narrow gauge main line.

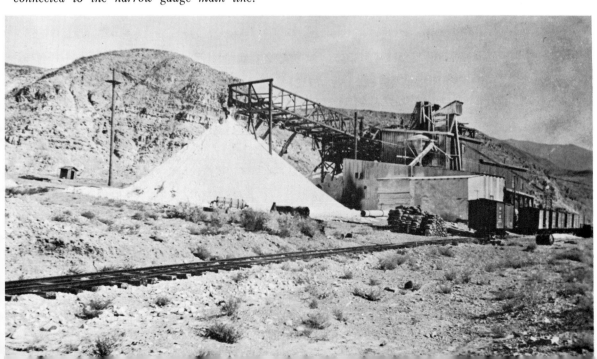

LILLIAN HILDERMAN COLLECTION

Failure of the grip lock (lower wheel and handle shown on bucket hanger) to hold the filled buckets on the cables resulted in part in the eventual abandonment of the tram in 1930.

Located 4 miles north of Keeler, the spur line to the salt mill can be seen to the right, in this early photo.

CARSON AND COLORADO RAILROAD.

TIME TABLE No. 7.

To take Effect on Sunday, January 1st, 1882, at 7.45 A. M.

For the Government and Information of Employés only.

1 Bodie and Candelaria EXPRESS.			Miles from Mound House.	STATIONS.		Miles from Belleville.		2 San Francisco & Virginia EXPRESS.	
..... 9.30	A. M. LV.		.... 0	Lv ..... **MOUND HOUSE** ..... Ar	6.0	.... 150 ...		..... 6.00	P. M. AR.
..... 10.00			.... 6	.... DAYTON	12.0	.... 144		..... 5.25	
..... 10.45			.... 18	.... CLIFTON	8.0	.... 132		..... 4.45	
..... 11.20			.... 26	.... FT. CHURCHILL........	2.0	... 124		..... 4.12	
..... 11.26			.... 28	.... WASHOUT........	10.0	.... 122		..... 4.05	
..... 12.00	M.		.... 38	.... WABUSKA............	4.0	.... 112		..... 3.25	
..... 12.15 ⎫ 12.30 ⎭	P. M.		.... 42	.... CLEAVER............	3.0	.... 108		..... 3.10	
..... 12.40			.... 45	.... MASON............	9.0	.... 105		..... 3.00	
..... 1.10			.. 54	.... RIO VISTA........	4.0	.... 96		..... 2.25	
..... 1.25			.... 58	.... RESERVATION............	7.0	.... 92		..... 2.10	
..... **1.47**			65	.... SCHURZ............	13.0	.... 85		..... **1.47**	
..... 2.30			.... 78	.... GILLIS............	22.0	.... 72		..... 1.00	P. M.
..... 3.40 ⎫ 4.10 ⎭			.... 100 ...	.... HAWTHORNE............	10.0	.... 50		..... 11.45 ⎫ 10.45 ⎭	
..... 4.43			.... 110	.... STANSFIELD....	3.2	.... 40		..... 10.05	
..... 4.53			.... 113	.... KINKEAD........	11.8	.... 36		..... 9.55	
..... 5.33			.... 125	.... LUNING............	6.0	.... 25		..... 9.15	
..... 5.56			.... 131	.... NEW BOSTON........	6.0	... 19		..... 8.55	
..... 6.15 ⎫ 6.30 ⎭			.... 137	.... SODA SPRINGS	6.0	... 13		..... 8.35	
..... 6.50			.... 143	.... RHODES	7.0	.... 7		..... 8.15	
..... 7.20	P. M. AR.		.... 150	Ar........ **BELLEVILLE**........ Lv		.... 0		..... 7.45	A. M. LV.

J. R. KING, Train Dispatcher, is authorized to move trains by Telegraph or otherwise.

Full Faced Figures denote meeting and passing places.   Trains run Daily.

The attention of Trainmen is particularly called to the Rules and Regulations printed on the back of this card, as they will be strictly enforced.

H. M. YERINGTON, Gen'l Supt.   W. H. CRISLER, Master Transportation.   R. J. LAWS, Asst. Supt.

RULES AND REGULATIONS FOR THE GOVERNMENT OF EMPLOYES.

SIGNALS.

1. A Red flag by day, a Red light by night, or an explosion of a torpedo on the track, is a signal of danger. A Red flag placed outside the rails signifies that the track is out of order, and speed of train or engine must be reduced to six miles per hour. A Red flag placed between the rails signifies that the track is impassable, and trains must come to a full stop.

2. A Red flag by day, or a Red light by night, displayed at a station, denotes that a telegram or train order is waiting, and the train must be brought to a stop.

3. One sound of the whistle is the signal to apply the brakes; two sounds of the whistle is the signal to let go the brakes; three sounds of the whistle is the signal to back; four sounds of the whistle is the signal to call in a flagman; several short sounds of the whistle is the signal of danger.

4. One stroke of the cab bell signifies stop. The cab bell *must not* be used to start trains.

5. A light swung over the head is a signal to go ahead; when swung across, or at right angles with the track, is a signal to back up; and when moved up and down is a signal to stop. If motion of lamp is quick, move quick (but with care); if slow, move slow.

6. Notice must be taken of all violent signals. Always stop and ascertain the meaning of every signal that may seem to indicate danger.

7. A Red flag by day, or a Red light by night, displayed on the front of an Engine, indicates that another Train is following, which has precisely the same rights as the Engine or Train bearing the signal.

8. All Night Trains (and Freight and Work Trains running in day time) must, in all cases, carry a Red signal on the rear car, and Engines running without Trains on rear of tender.

RUNNING RULES.

9. Train bound south will have the right to the track against Train moving in opposite direction, until it (the Train bound south) is thirty minutes behind its card (leaving) time; after which, the Train bound north will have the right to the track indefinitely, as against Train moving in opposite direction, keeping thirty minutes behind its card (leaving) time, at each and every succeeding Station, until the expected Train is met.

10. Always allow five minutes for possible variation of watches. Time must be compared daily with clock in Mound House office, which will be considered standard time.

11. Construction and Extra Trains must keep at least five minutes out of the way of all Time Table Trains. South-bound Trains will take side track when practicable.

12. All Trains will approach terminal Stations with great care. Conductors of Trains and Engineers of Engines, running without Trains, will register at terminal stations, in a book kept for that purpose, the time of their arrival and departure.

13. Conductors of all Trains, immediately before starting out on their runs, will go in person to the Telegraph Office, to inquire if any special orders are awaiting them.

GENERAL RULES.

14. No person will be allowed to ride free.

15. No person employed on Trains or at Stations will be allowed to leave his position or change with another, without permission from the General or Assistant Superintendent.

16. Trains will be under the control of the Conductor, and will be run as nearly on card time as possible; although the Conductor has charge of the Train, the Engineer will not be considered blameless if he runs any unnecessary risks.

17. Train men will consult Bulletin Boards daily.

18. The use of intoxicating drinks is strictly forbidden, and the use of them while on duty will be deemed sufficient cause for dismissal from the service of the Company.

19. Conductors or Brakemen of *all* Trains meeting or passing, or when approaching a Station, *must be out* looking for signals, and be prepared to do anything required for safety or expedition; and all Trainmen will be at their Train at least fifteen minutes before starting time, and examine the same to see if everything is in order.

20. Conductors will report in writing to the General or Assistant Superintendent all injuries to persons caused by their Train, giving number of Train and Engine; the names of all employes on their Train; also, the names of others witnessing accident, and all other information that may be useful as a matter of record, and, whenever practicable, get the signatures of employes and other witnesses to report, after reading the same to them. In case of accident, resulting in injury to passengers or employes, or damage to rolling stock or contents of cars, the Conductor (if Conductor is disabled, the head Brakeman) will immediately notify the General or Assistant Superintendent by telegraph of such accident, giving full particulars, and stating what assistance, if any, is required.

21. IN NO CASE MUST A CAR BE LEFT ON A GRADE WITHOUT THE BRAKE BEING SET AND THE WHEELS BLOCKED. Conductors of Freight and Work Trains, in switching out cars at Stations, or meeting and passing Trains on tracks where station work is done, should leave cars, as near as practicable, as they find them, or at convenient places for loading or unloading. They will also render Station Agents assistance in switching cars, in order to an economical disposition of the business of Stations.

22. Conductors will have the names of Stations announced in all passenger cars.

23. Conductors will see that switches, after being used, are left turned to the main track. Any employe leaving a switch turned from the main track, or unlocked, after using, will be dismissed from the service of the Company.

24. A Brakeman must be stationed on rear car, and not leave his position without permission from his Conductor.

25. Brakemen must not slip the wheels, and it is the duty of the Conductor to see to this matter.

26. No section or other Foreman will allow his hand car to be used on the track, except in the service of the Company.

27. Engineers or Firemen should look back frequently to see that all is right; and in case the Train has broken apart, GREAT CARE must be taken to keep the forward end out of the way of detached part; sounding whistle repeatedly to warn Trainmen, and if on a down grade, the forward part of the Train will KEEP MOVING, EVEN TO THE NEXT STATION, IF NECESSARY. If detached portion or Train is out of sight, and it is necessary to back up, before doing so, if on a down grade, allow ample time to elapse before starting, and send a man back with flag at least fifteen (15) minutes before moving; and if there is no Brakeman on top of Train, after flag has been sent back, the Engineer will send his Fireman out on Train to keep watch and give necessary signals; then move with great care, stopping at all obscure places, unless it is certain that rear part of Train is at a stand and will not move until reached. Every precaution must be used to prevent accidents. TAKE NO CHANCES.

28. Dampers of Ash Pans must in all cases be closed while Engines are crossing bridges and wood yards.

29. Engineers will not allow any person to ride on Engine, except officers of Company and Foremen of Track.

30. Great care must be taken to prevent killing live stock. BRING THE TRAIN TO A FULL STOP IF NECESSARY. Should any be killed or struck, the Engineer must report in writing, on blanks furnished for that purpose, to General or Assistant Superintendent, giving number of Engine, number of Train, names of Conductor and Fireman, and all other information that may be useful.

31. Station Agents are required to see that the doors of all cars on the side tracks are securely fastened, and that the brakes are set, and the cars far enough from the main track as not to endanger passing Trains, and that the wheels of all cars on side tracks are properly blocked, and cars must NEVER be allowed TO STAND ON THE MAIN TRACK.

32. In all cases, either by day or night, when the track is obstructed, by reason of repairing or otherwise, so as to endanger the passing of Trains, a Red flag by day or a Red light by night must be placed at least three-quarters of a mile in both directions, so as to be plainly seen by an approaching train. Road Masters will see that Section Men are on hand during stormy weather and time of flood, to properly guard the track and bridges from water and slides.

32. Engineers must sound the whistle at all obscure places, and ring bell at cosssings.

RULES GOVERNING THE MOVEMENT OF TRAINS BY TELEGRAPH.

34. No more than one person shall be permitted to move trains by special orders, at the same time. The General or Assistant Superintendent, and such other person as he may designate as "TRAIN DISPATCHER," shall be authorized to move Trains by Telegraph, or otherwise. Train Dispatchers will closely watch all Trains, both on and off of time, AND ANTICIPATE THEIR WANTS, that no time may be lost at Telegraph Stations waiting for orders.

35. All special orders and messages involving the movement of Trains shall be communicated in writing, and addressed to the Conductor and Engineer of the Train, and shall be *positive and defined*. The Conductor shall write his understanding of the order, which shall be read to the Engineer and signed by both, which must in all cases be repeated back to the dispatching office, and the Dispatcher, if correctly understood, will telegraph back O. K. Operators will in no case sign the names of Conductor or Engineer, to their understanding of the order. All orders and messages in regard to the movement of Trains must be written in full, and no abbreviations shall be used, except 12 (how do you understand) or 13 (I understand; I am to). Operators will not suffer an order to leave their possession until they have received and endorsed upon the same, O. K., in answer to the 13 message of Conductor and Engineer, nor until they have signed the same.

36. Conductors of Work Trains, must notify Train Dispatcher in the evening, between what points they will work the next day, and get their orders; should it become necessary to go outside of those limits, they will proceed with great caution, and at the first telegraph office, ask Train Dispatcher to extend the limits as provided in Rule 35. Their working hours will be from 6 A. M. to 7 P. M.; should they wish to work earlier or later, they must get special order to do so.

37. In all cases where trains are run by special orders, either by telegraph or writing, the orders will specify the Trains to which they refer, and the special orders will not affect Trains or Engines which may be following the leading Trains, unless such following Trains or Engines are *distinctly* stated in special orders.

38. Under no circumstances accept verbal orders for the movement of trains.

39. When an operator receives an order to hold a Train, he must first put out a Red flag or Red light; then give his understanding of the order; a written copy of such order for holding the train must be made and delivered to the Conductor, who will show the same to the Engineer; he will be careful to observe that the signal is not disturbed or hidden, and will notify all other Trains that the signal is not for them. The red signal must not be relied upon exclusively to hold Trains; operators are expected to watch closely for the expected Train, using all necessary means to stop it.

40. Should a Train be held at a Telegraph Station where there is no night operator, the Conductor may call the day operator into the office to get orders for him.

Main Street, Candelaria, Nevada, 1893; view is looking West. The C&C station was situated beyond the hill to the extreme left of the photo. With the devaluation of silver ore, the place was now starting to become a "ghost town."

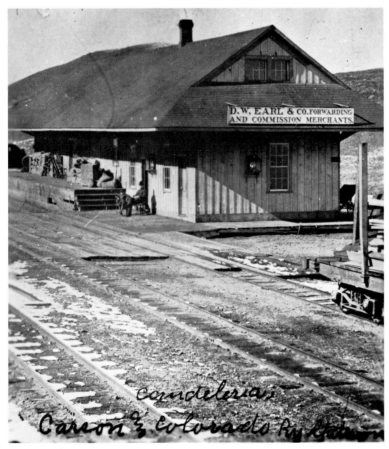

By 1894, traffic at the Candelaria station was at a standstill. Passenger tickets were for one way — out!

Pass *J. N. McBride*

Roadmaster

— OVER —

CARSON & COLORADO RAILWAY

1893 UNLESS OTHERWISE ORDERED.

UNTIL DECEMBER 31ST 1893

No. 20

PRES'T AND GEN'T SUP'T

LITH. BRITTON & REY S.F.

CARSON & COLORADO RAILWAY COMPANY.
— CONDITIONS —

The person accepting this Free Ticket assumes all risk of accidents, and expressly agrees that the Company shall not be liable under any circumstances, whether of negligence by their Agents, or otherwise for injury of the Person, or for loss or injury to the Property of the passenger using this Ticket.

If presented by any other person than the individual named thereon, the Conductor will take up this Ticket and collect fares.   I fully accept the above conditions.

J. N. McBride

Sign in ink.

1920   FOR MERIT   No. A 25789

Southern Pacific Company

Pass --- Mr. R.L. Gracey ---

Account   Agent

Between All stations on Salt Lake Div.-

UNTIL DECEMBER 31st 1920 { UNLESS OTHERWISE ORDERED AND
VALID WHEN COUNTERSIGNED BY C. J. MILLIS { SUBJECT TO CONDITIONS ON BACK

COUNTERSIGNED BY

Wm Sproule
PRESIDENT.

SOUTHERN PACIFIC COMPANY
PACIFIC SYSTEMS

ORDER FOR EMPLOYEE RATE

Agent S. P. Co. at Initial Point:

Sell the ticket described herein to the person named, and at the Employee's Rate, if issued according to the regulations on the reverse side hereof and countersigned by:

W. S. PALMER, Gen. Supt. Northern District, or R. E. MONTGOMERY, Chief Clerk.

R. H. INGRAM, Gen. Supt. Southern District, or P. J. ARCHER, Chief Clerk.

W. R. SCOTT, Supt., A. W. BAKER, Asst. Supt., or T. LOVE, Chief Clerk.

T. R. JONES, Supt., H. B. BRECKENFELD, Asst. Supt., or J. J. HENDERSON, Chief Clerk.

E. C. MANSON, Supt., or J. F. SHAUGHNESSY, Asst. Supt.

J. C. WILDER, Supt., E. R. ANTHONY, Asst. Supt., or H. R. HICKS, Chief Clerk.

D. BURKHALTER, Supt., W. H. AVERELL, Asst. Supt., or C. S. Green, Chief Clerk.

H. V. PLATT, Supt., T. McCAFFERY, Asst. Supt., or A. M. SMITH, Chief Clerk.

W. A. McGOVERN, Supt., or W. D. BEUHRING, Chief Clerk.

For Mrs. *Lottie Brendarsing*

Employee of *Family   Agent*
(Office or Department.)

From *Mina*

To *Laws*

NOT GOOD ON ANY LIMITED TRAIN.

Kind of Ticket *____*   Rate *____*

Order void after *Jan 31* 190*6*

COUNTERSIGNED:
(See other side.)

J H Goodman
GEN. PASS. AND TICKET AGENT.

SIGNATURE OF EMPLOYEE OR PERSON FOR WHOM ISSUED:

Form 702

3185 B

Keeler	SWANSEA	INYO	MT. WHITNEY	OWENYO	FRANCIS	CITRUS	ABERDEEN	ELNA	ALVORD	BLACK CANYON	BIGELOW	POLITA	LAWS	CHALFANT	MILLNER	HAMMIL	BENTON	STATE LINE	QUEEN	SILEX	SUMMIT	BASALT

AGENT'S STUB.   DIVISION OUTWARD.   Form 65

If an Half

INSTRUCTIONS TO AGENT.

Stamp ticket and stub for actual date of sale.

Fold the ticket and indicate destination on ticket and stub with one impression of punch.

Punch ½ on ticket and stub if sold as an half ticket.

If destination be not printed hereon, write it with pen and ink in a bold heavy hand across both destination columns.

½ Fare Ticket Punch Here.

AGENT MUST RETAIN THIS STUB.

3932 A

Mound House	DAYTON	CORDELLI	SPUR "A"	CLIFTON	LYON	TUCELA	FT. CHURCHILL	SPUR "B"	WABUSKA	PENROSE	CLEAVER	MASON	RIO VISTA	SCHURZ	CILLIS	Hawthorne	KINKEAD	LUNING	NEW BOSTON	SODAVILLE	RHODES	BELLEVILLE	"JUNCTION"	Candelaria

GEORGE TURNER COLLECTION

The "Belleville," engine No. 5, coals up at the Laws hoist. Traces of the facility still were evident 60-odd years after this photo was taken.

Shade was always at a minimum on the route of the "Princess." Here the crew and engine No. 4 take a breather at Hammil in 1917.

T. L. WILLIAMSON COLLECTION

11

L. K. RALSTON

This could well be the last photo taken of the Hawthorne passenger station, as it was taken on Aug. 5, 1905, one week prior to its dismantling. Shown left to right: L. K. Ralston, agent; the "Sky Pilot;" Frank Taylor, brakeman.

MRS. AUSTIN ROBERTS

From various reports, the departure time for the Hawthorne stage-coach, shown here, was somewhat more flexible than the advertisement indicates.

A rare view indeed is this panorama of Hawthorne taken prior to 1900, from atop the water pump derrick.

E. F. BOX COLLECTION

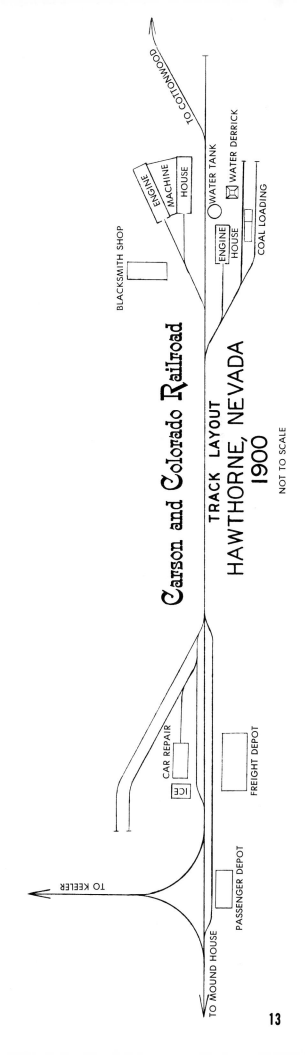

Carson and Colorado Railroad

TRACK LAYOUT
HAWTHORNE, NEVADA
1900

NOT TO SCALE

TO COTTONWOOD

BLACKSMITH SHOP

ENGINE
MACHINE
HOUSE

WATER TANK

WATER DERRICK

ENGINE
HOUSE

COAL LOADING

CAR REPAIR

ICE

FREIGHT DEPOT

TO KEELER

PASSENGER DEPOT

TO MOUND HOUSE

Here's one slip that really showed . . . which perhaps was one reason that the "Bodie" was the first of the original C&C engines to be scrapped in 1907.

.....Nobody's Perfect!

C&C No. 8 huffs and puffs a sigh of relief after being re-railed at the turn of the century. A stubborn (and now dead) cow munching grass was the cause of the temporary delay.

14

1

All was well with engine No. 5 at Mt. Montgomery station on July 23, 1923; engine No. 8 was later coupled to No. 5 prior to leaving for the south.

2

A short time later descending into California, the lead engine derailed and the results are shown here.

Asst Supt H.W.Wistner in gangway wearin straw h

3

After the pieces were picked up, the crippled 4-4-0's pause for a breather enroute to Mina for repairs.

On a cold February day in 1937, the crew and engine No. 22 "freeze" for the camera, while pondering their predicament.

Icy track near Benton proved to be too slippery for S.P. No. 1 on this December day in 1931.

Engine No. 14 becomes No. "41" as a result of this derailment near Basalt.

The need for additional motive power during the Tonopah Bonanza resulted in several engines being loaned to the C&C. Here the San Joaquin & Sierra Nevada R.R. No. 1026 gets a fresh load of coal at Hawthorne in 1901.

Shown in 1924, engine No. 10 illustrates the effects of impromptu rework. Domes are from different eras, the tender is a wood-to-oil conversion, and parentage of the headlamp is anyone's guess!

RAILROAD TIME TABLE.

CARSON AND COLORADO R. R.

Taking Effect
FEBRUARY 10, 1883.

First Division.

BODIE AND CANDELARIA EXPRESS:

Stations.	Bodie and Candelaria.	San Fran'co and Virginia
Mound House	9:30 a. m.	6:00 p. m.
Dayton	10:00 a. m.	5:25 p. m.
Clifton	10:45 a. m.	4:45 p. m.
Fort Churchill	11:20 a. m.	4:12 p. m.
Washout	11:26 a. m.	4:05 p. m.
Wabuska	12:00 m.	3:35 p. m.
Cleaver	12:15 p. m. 12:30 p. m.	3:10 p. m. 2:55 p. m.
Mason	12:40 p. m.	2:45 p. m.
Rio Vista	1:06 p. m.	2:12 p. m.
Reservation	1:20 p. m.	2:00 p. m.
Schurz	1:40 p. m.	1:40 p. m.
Gillis	2:30 p. m.	12:50 p. m.
Hawthorne	3:40 p. m. 4:10 p. m.	11:40 a. m. 11:00 a. m.
Stansfield	4:43 p. m.	10:30 a. m.
Kinkead	4:53 p. m.	10:20 a. m.
Luning	5:33 p. m.	9:35 a. m.
New Boston	5:56 p. m.	9:15 a. m.
Soda Springs	6:15 p. m. 6:30 p. m.	8:55 a. m. 8:35 a. m.
Rhodes	6:50 p. m.	8:15 a. m.
Belleville	7:20 p. m.	7:45 a. m.
Junction	7:30 p. m.	7:35 a. m.
Candelaria	8:00 p. m.	7:00 a. m.

Second Division.

BELLEVILLE AND BENTON EXPRESS.

Stations.	Benton Express.	Belleville Express.
Belleville	7:00 p. m.	7:55 a. m.
Junction	7:10 p. m. 7:30 p. m.	7:45 a. m. 7:30 a. m.
Basalt	6:00 a. m.	8:45 p. m.
Summit	5:05 a. m.	9:25 p. m.
Queen	4:15 a. m.	10:25 p. m.
Benton	3:30 a. m.	11:15 p. m.

The above trains are run daily and make close connection at Mound House with trains of the Virginia and Truckee railroad for Virginia City and Reno, and with the Central Pacific at Reno, via the Virginia and Truckee, for all points East and West.

Stage Connections:

At Hawthorne with the United States Stage Company's coaches for Aurora, (25 miles); Bodie, (37 miles); Lundy and Bridgeport.

At Luning (125 miles from Mound House) with Gilmer, Salisbury & Co.'s tri-weekly stages leaving Mondays, Wednesdays and Fridays for Downeyville, Grantsville and Belmont.

At Candelaria with the stages for Columbus (8 miles), Silver Peak, Montezuma, Lida Valley, Gold Mountain, etc.

At Benton with daily stages for Bishop Creek, Independence, Cerro Gordo, etc.

H. M. YERINGTON, Gen. Supt.
R. J. LAWS, Assistant Superintendent.
D. A. BENDER,
General Freight and Passenger Agent.

Narrow gauge locomotives used the left portion of the Mina engine house and also shared some trackage on the right. In this 1906 photo former C&C engines No. 3, 5, 10 & 11 had recently been re-lettered for the N&C.

Living space was at a premium at Mina in 1905 during the standard gauge operations of the line. Mrs. Church, sister of Superintendent Laws, is shown here as a resident of "Cartown," set up in the Mina yards from converted box cars.

View looking south of the Mina yards in busier days gone by. A portion of the transfer trestle can be seen to the left, with "Cartown" extending toward the engine house.

Triple heading was normal daily procedure for those consists scheduled to make the run over Mt. Montgomery. Engines No. 12, 16 and 18 pause in 1931 before leaving the Mina yards.

Waiting inside the Mina engine house are engines No. 8 and 14 in 1932.

At a 7,138 foot elevation, Mt. Montgomery station represented a fair climb on anyone's railroad!

T. L. WILLIAMSON COLLECTION

R. AHRNKE

Always a popular "photo stop" was the California-Nevada border. Here #8 and crew pause before heading South.

. . . the middle of "nowhar" . . . Basalt stood alone, as this scene shows, taken from atop the water tower. Track at top left swings toward Mina.

For many years Wabuska was a busy station, as it was also the Junction point for the Nevada Copper Belt R.R.

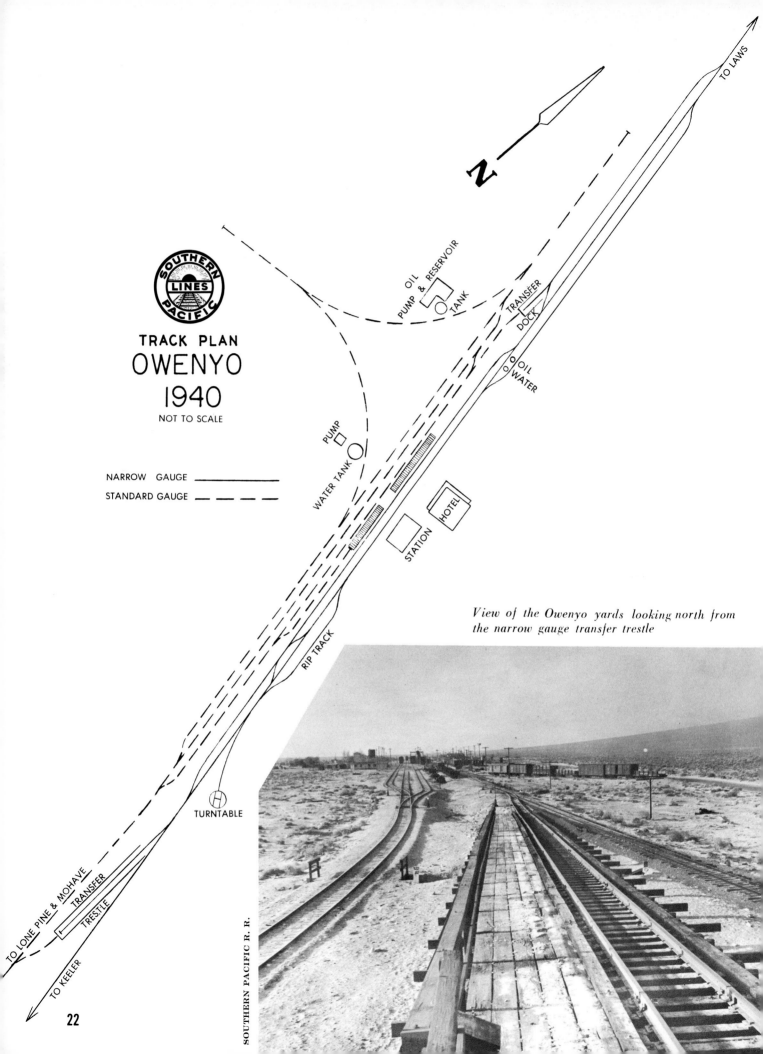

SOUTHERN
PACIFIC
LINES

TRACK PLAN
OWENYO
1940
NOT TO SCALE

NARROW GAUGE _____
STANDARD GAUGE _ _ _ _ _ _ _

N

TO LAWS

OIL & RESERVOIR

PUMP TANK

TRANSFER DOCK

OIL
WATER

PUMP

WATER TANK

HOTEL

STATION

RIP TRACK

TURNTABLE

TO LONE PINE & MOHAVE

TRANSFER TRESTLE

TO KEELER

22

View of the Owenyo yards looking north from the narrow gauge transfer trestle

SOUTHERN PACIFIC R. R.

Flying high at Owenyo, No. 9 discharges her ore into the standard gauge cars in the "basement."

Owenyo . . . in busier days

A *"condensed Princess" switches at Owenyo in 1938.*

The "Little Giant" ambles past Monola Siding in 1959; her consist typical of those runs that preceded the final curtain for the road.

Thirst in the desert was common to men and engines alike . . . Here the Kearsarge water tower obliges engine No. 8 in 1951.

Long a familiar figure on the Keeler branch, W. C. Ferguson is shown at the throttle of Diesel No. 1. His unexpected passing shortly after the line was dismantled was a great loss to the diminishing fraternity of narrow gauge engineers.

EASTWARD

Capacity of siding, car lengths	SECOND CLASS 190 Mixed Lv. Tuesday Thursday Saturday	SECOND CLASS 194 Mixed Lv. Monday Wednesday Friday	FIRST CLASS 24 Tonopah Express Mixed Leave Daily	Distance from San Francisco	STATIONS Time Table No. 41 September 27, 1931 Mina Branch	Distance from Mina	FIRST CLASS 23 San Francisco Passenger Mixed Arrive Daily	THIRD CLASS 189 Mixed Ar. Monday Wednesday Friday	THIRD CLASS 193 Mixed Lv. Tuesday Thursday Saturday
Yard TWPBK	9.15AM	11.40PM	11.40PM	288.1	HAZEN TO-R	128.9	s 2.45AM		s 4.00PM
47	f 9.25	11.50PM	292.9	BANGO 2.8	124.1	f 2.35		f 3.40	
			f	295.9	LAHONTAN 1.0	121.8	f 2.35		
Spur 13		f	296.2	1.7	120.8	f			
Spur 85			12.01AM	297.9	LAMAR RUGBY 4.6	119.1	f 2.25		f 3.30
46	f 9.35	f 12.01AM	297.9	HAWES 4.0	114.6	f 2.15		f 3.17
46	f 9.45	f 12.11	302.5	APPIAN 1.4	110.0	f 2.05		f 3.03
46 W	f 9.58	f 12.25	307.0	PAWNEE 4.7	104.5	f 1.50		f 2.48
47	f 10.10	f 12.35	813.5	WEEKS 2.6	108.2	f		
10		f 12.40	816.4	CHURCHILL 11.1	108.2	f		
76 POY	12.20PM	R 827.5	N.C.B. CROSSING 0.3	100.6	s 1.00PM	f 2.40		
Yard PYW	s 12.45PM	s 10.45AM	1.15	828.0	WABUSKA 4.8	89.2	s 1.15		f 3.40
3		f	TO-R 831.9	LUX 2.7	85.1	s 12.35PM	f 2.15PM	
27		f 1.35	384.6	MOQUIST 9.1	82.4	f 12.10PM		
28 P		f 1.55	848.7	RIO VISTA 4.0	73.8	f 11.50PM		
33		f 2.05	847.7	RESERVATION 1.6	69.8	f 11.40		
Spur 4		849.3	ZAIS 4.4	67.7				
66 W		s 2.20	854.2	SCHURZ 7.2 TO	62.8	s 11.20		
34		f 3.00	861.4	STUCKEY 5.9	55.8	f 10.57		
26 P		f 3.15	367.8	GILLIS 2.0	49.7	f 10.45		
Spur 2 P		f	369.3	NOLAN 0.3	47.7	f 10.40		
35 P		f 3.35	376.6	MAGNUS 2.0	40.4	f 10.25		
24		f 3.40	878.6	WALKER 5.6	38.2			
46	s 3.55	884.4 TO	THORNE 5.0	32.6	s 10.10		
47	f 4.50	889.4	DOVER 0.6	27.6	f 9.41		
37		f 394.0	KINKEAD 7.1	23.0	f 9.31		
33 P		f 401.1	ACME 7.1	15.9			
41		s 408.2	LUNING 8.8	8.8	f 9.04		
Yard POYBK	s 5.55AM	s 5.30	417.0	MINA 0.0	0.0	8.45PM		

Keeler Station after the turn of the century, with a former South Pacific Coast box car standing by.

"Keep digging, there's a roadbed down there somewhere" . . . The result of a "little" rain at Keeler in 1919.

27

Formerly the Bodie & Benton mogul "Mono," the Inyo Development Company engine No. 1 is shown at work at Keeler in 1904.

This complacent view of the Keeler station looks south toward the Panamint Mountains

...*Home stretch!*

FRED HUST

Here is a good example of an "open shop" . . . engine facilities at Keeler, California provided plenty of fresh air for the mechanics!

GEORGE TURNER COLLECTION

Boom Town With A
Silver Lining Was....

GEORGE TURNER COLLECTION

Discovered in 1865, the Cerro Gordo Mine and town still boasted many buildings in 1917. The American Hotel is shown at lower right; main mine buildings are in the center; the upper tramway terminus is shown at left center.

CERRO GORDO

GEORGE TURNER

Inside the mine hoist building is located the main shaft, where it is reported that several Chinese miners are still buried from an early day cave in.

Equipment contained within the Cerro Gordo mine buildings is still operable and only awaits the twist of Fate to start a new hum of activity.

EASTERN CALIFORNIA MUSEUM

The silver bars shown gleaming in the desert sun represented a portion of the $213,392,000 produced from 1880 to 1948 by the Cerro Gordo mines.

Built in 1915, the Cerro Gordo tramway was oper-ated until 1927. For the next 33 years, the ore buckets (some still full) quietly hung as silent sentinels reminiscent of the bonanza passed.

Here empty cars await the turning of the tram cable wheels at the Keeler terminus . . . in vain, as the tramway was dismantled in 1960. It was transported bolt and board to Candelaria, Nevada to participate in a modern day mining promotion.

Representing the actual 'end' of the S.P. narrow gauge was the Natural Soda Products Company, some two miles south of Keeler, California, in this photo taken in 1948.

34

Ghost Rails To Oblivion

Surely as the desert sands will shift, so did the rails of the "Slim Princess." Changes in the national economy coupled with related local conditions quite naturally fathered alterations in the right-of-way. Although the Carson & Colorado operated on a course of continual decline, it never experienced an abandonment during its corporate existence.

After transfer to Southern Pacific ownership, the inevitable plague of all narrow gauge roads set in . . . "Dismantling Fever" . . . the first victim being the 7.3 miles of rail comprising the Cottonwood Branch, south from Hawthorne, Nevada, in 1902. Ironically, this was the only 'expansion' the C&C had ever established.

1905 proved to be a banner year for changes. In order to overcome the freight tieup problems at Mound House due to gauge differences, the rails to Tonopah Junction were widened. Included was the addition of 28 miles of track connecting Churchill to the S.P. main line at Hazen, Nevada. Thus, through rail service on standard gauge track was provided, eliminating the services of the Virginia & Truckee for such service. In turn, the town of Hawthorne was completely by-passed during the broad gauging and the slim rails were removed. Further south,

the Candelaria Branch also fell in the 1905 'wave' of abandonments. Not that such action wasn't warranted, as Candelaria was practically a ghost town by the turn of the century. Both the Hawthorne and Candelaria passenger stations were razed in 1905. The Hawthorne freight depot still continued to do business with wagons to Bodie, and today houses the local Elks Club. To round out the 1905 realignments, three-rail track was laid between Mina and Tonopah Junction. This enabled the dwindling S.P. narrow gauge to provide through service for the newly established Tonopah R.R. with connections at Mina.

After enjoying a thirty year period of operations in a casual manner when the majority of the nation's slim rails had become memories, the "fever" struck again. By now, the remaining 168 miles were an easy target for abandonment. With the country in the depth of a depression, who needed the extra expense of an obsolete division connecting two large sandpiles??

The first section of rail to be abandoned in 1934 was the seldom-used track between Mound House and Churchill. Candelaria proved to be much harder to get rid of . . . this branch was "reabandoned" in 1931 but the rails were not finally taken up until 1934. Intermittent mining activity in the Candelaria mountains had called upon the services of the railroad occasionally, even though it was "officially" abandoned in 1905. In 1936 the track was dismantled from Mound House to Churchill. The rails from Tonopah Junction, Nevada to Benton, California followed suit in abandonment during 1938. Actual removal of the light iron did not take place until the abandonment of the Benton to Laws trackage in 1943.

Had the Southern Pacific delayed the final abandonment and last run of the narrow gauge by just 11 days, the road would have been able to celebrate its eightieth birthday. In startling contrast to all of the previous liesurely abandonments, the ink was hardly dry on the last train orders of April 29, 1960, when the first rails were uprooted. Bulldozers were busy in Keeler that morning clearing a roadway for asphalt pavement. Truck service was replacing the rail service at one end as spike-pulling ceremonies were being formulated at the other, in Laws.

So swift was action taken that the rail was removed across the road at Zurich by the High-way Department before the salvage equipment was assembled. This condition required the contractor to forego the use of the train for normal rail removal between Laws and Zurich.

Today, scattered ties, numerous spikes, water tower foundations and tie plates can still be found along the right of way south from Mina. The Mt. Montgomery tunnel is still accessible and can be reached by automobile. Stone linings of the enginehouse pit and turntable are in evidence at Candelaria. A mixed consist coupled behind engine #9 deteriorates at the Laws station under the guise of a County Park. This is little enough to mark the four score years of gentle achievement and casual accomplishment of one of America's true Bonanza Railroads . . . the setting sun will never rise again to the sound of steam blowing through the desert sands in the wake of the Slim Princess.

Shown is a portion of the ties removed as a result of the abandonment of the Tonopah Junction to Benton section during 1943.

This rare photo recorded in part the dismantling of the Candelaria Station during September of 1905.

The N. G. #9 is scheduled to be hauled dead to

Laws, Calif.   **on**   APR 2 5 1960

account reported donated to the city of Bishop.

The last run of the N. G. will be on   APR 2 9 1960

when all cars will be brought in from

KEELER, CALIF. and   Laws, Calif.

and the line abandoned.   Southern Pacific Co,
                          R. E. Cartt - Agent
                          Owenyo, Calif.

The last word is issued in this simple notice and the Keeler Branch is no more . . .

GEORGE TURNER

The "Grand Old Lady," engine No. 9, rides a free pass on her last trip. Having failed to pass an I.C.C. boiler inspection earlier, No. 9 was deprived of making her last run by her own power.

Bringing a close to an 80 year history, the last train from Keeler is about to depart on April 29, 1960. A bulldozer is already at work on a replacement roadway . . . of asphalt.

It is entirely possible that the remains shown here went on to become a part of an object in an outer space project . . . !

No abandonment is complete without a fitting ceremony. Supt. R. R. Robinson of the S.P. San Joaquin Division officiates for the pulling of the "first" spike at Laws station.

These men shared the honors of serving as the last crew of the Slim Princess on April 29, 1960. Left to right: Bob Cartt, Agent; Bob Olson, Brakeman; Jerry Jones, Brakeman; G. C. McGhee, Conductor; W. C. "Furgie" Furguson, Engineer and Mr. Graves, Fireman.

Just south of Laws, trucks substitute for the scrap train. Premature removal of a section of track at Zurich prevented customary removal of rail.

Preceeding the track removal, the spike puller at times required an assist on stubborn spikes that had become fused to the ties.

GEORGE TURNER

The first portion of the Keeler Branch rail that was removed is loaded at Zurich in September, 1960.

The track gang keeps a steady pace as the scrap train nears Kearsarge.

GEORGE TURNER

INYO REGISTER, Bishop, California

41

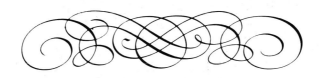

Modeler's Portfolio

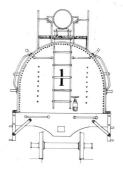

Presenting prototype plans and photos that may be used to reconstruct the Carson & Colorado - S. P. narrow gauge in miniature.

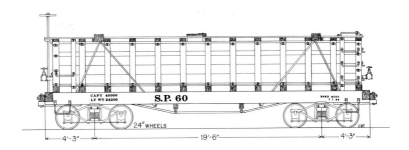

Logging was never predominant on the C&C (except for the short-lived Cottonwood Branch). This does not rule out this theme, as timber for mining activites and fuel for the early wood-burners were necessities. The tranquility in the logging town of Bullfrog is depicted above on the HOn3 layout of Hank Johnston.

Model Railroading as a hobby provides an excellent diversion from the tensions created in our "Space Age." The very nature of railroad operation is in stark contrast to the race to the Moon. A narrow gauge division or complete layout further enhances the hobby by providing a very nostalgic era to model. Selecting the Carson & Colorado - S. P. prototype will afford one great flexibility in construction of rolling stock, as many modifications in cars were made throughout the road's history.

Aside from the original eight 4-4-0 locomotives purchased in the 80's, no new steam equipment ran on the slim rails of the line. Abandonments or broad gauging of other roads provided a ready supply of motive power when needed. This condition eventually resulted in many changes in appearance of the engines due to repair or replacement of parts. Gradual change to the use of oil caused boiler and tender rework. Headlamps, smokestacks, steam and sand domes were replaced piecemeal during overhaul. It would be difficult to depict the many variations any one engine showed from original use to retirement. Attempts to compile a definitive list of every engine that was assigned to the line after Southern Pacific ownership have been somewhat futile to date.

Passenger and freight equipment followed in the same vein as did the engines. Most of the new C&C equipment was built in the Central Pacific shops and showed a marked resemblance in car styling to the C.P. During the Tonopah 'boom,' additional freight equipment was badly needed and was obtained from the South Pacific Coast R.R. and the Nevada-California-Oregon. This condition in later years produced a lineage of many sizes and shapes. It would be rather difficult, for example, to classify any one style of freight or passenger truck as "exact prototype."

The plans shown represent some of the more interesting pieces of equipment that were used during the life of the road. Dimensions given do not necessarily apply to any other car of a like type . . . there being no reason to "standardize." In an attempt to furnish the clearest information possible, the plans are reproduced in as large a scale as the page would allow. Adapting the plans to personal use can be easily accomplished with the aid of a Model Railroad Reference Scale.

CARSON & COLORADO NARROW GAUGE R. R. LOCOMOTIVE ROSTER

RAILROAD ENGINE NUMBERS					TYPE	DATE IN SERVICE	BUILDER	SERIAL NUMBER	CYLINDERS	DRIVERS	WEIGHT		TRACTIVE EFFORT	BOILER PRESSURE (lbs.)	DISPOSITION
C&C	N&C	SPC	NCO	SP							ON DRIVERS	OF ENGINE			
1	1				4-4-0	Oct 1880	Baldwin	5285	14x18	41"	32,000	48,000	8520		Sold to Eureka & Palisade R.R., April 20, 1907
			14	1	2-8-0	Apr 1919	Baldwin	41300	17x20	40"	84,000	94,000	22110	180	Purchased from NCO 1928. Sold to N.C.N.G. 1933 (#9)
			1		2-4-0	Dec 1891			10x14	35"	23,000	32,650	4250		
			1		Diesel	Oct 1954	Genl. Elec.	32226			102,000	102,000	25500		Sold to Pan American Engineering Co., April, 1961
2	2				4-4-0	Feb 1881	Baldwin	5428	14x18	41"	32,000	48,000	8520		Scrapped July 31, 1907
			2		2-4-0	Dec 1891	Ricks & Frith		10x14	35"	23,000	32,650	4250		
3	3				4-4-0	Feb 1881	Baldwin	5430	14x18	44"	32,000	48,000	8520		Scrapped Sept. 23, 1908
		3			4-4-0	Aug 1887	Baldwin	8791	12x18	44"		41,600	6660	130	Scrapped Sept. 1934
4	4				4-6-0	Sep 1881	Baldwin	5782	14x18	44"	32,000	48,000	9540	140	Sold to N.C.N.G. June 6, 1929 (#7)
			4		4-6-0	Oct 1899	Baldwin	17124	15x18	44"		72,690	12500	160	Scrapped, 1934
5	5				4-4-0	Apr 1882	Baldwin	6089	14x18	43"	32,000	48,000	9760	140	Scrapped, January 20, 1932
			5		4-6-0	Nov 1899	Baldwin	17123	15x18	44"		72,690	12500	160	Scrapped, 1934
6	6				4-4-0	Apr 1882	Baldwin	6090	14x18	44"	32,000	48,000	9760	140	Scrapped, July 31, 1907
			6		4-6-0	Apr 1903	Baldwin	22020	15x20	44"		72,690	12500	160	Scrapped, 1934
		6			4-4-0	Jun 1877	Baldwin	4223	12x18	44"	29,000	45,500	6510	130	Operated Mina to Keeler, 1917-21. Scrapped 1926
7	7				4-4-0	Apr 1883	Baldwin	6687	14x18	43"	32,000	48,000	9760	140	Scrapped, January 20, 1932
			7		4-6-0	Apr 1903	Baldwin	22012	15x20	44"	72,690	92,500	12500	160	Scrapped, 1935
		8			4-4-0	Apr 1883	Baldwin	6689	14x18	44"	32,000	48,000	9540	140	Scrapped, February 10, 1932
			8		4-6-0	Aug 1907	Baldwin	31445	16x20	44"	62,000	81,000	17800	180	Donated to Carson City, Nevada, May 5, 1955
9	9				4-4-0	Jun 1885	Baldwin	7604	15x18	49"	33,000	52,000	9840	140	Scrapped Feb. 10, 1911
			9	16	4-6-0	Nov 1909	Baldwin	34035	16x20	44"	71,000	87,150	17880	180	Came from NCO 1928. Donated to City of Bishop, 1960
10		17			4-4-0	Jun 1885	Baldwin	7605	15x18	51"	33,000	52,000	9110	135	Scrapped, April 20, 1933
11		11			4-6-0	Jun 1881	Baldwin	5649	14x18	45"	57,000	73,600	9330	140	Rebuilt from 2-6-0, 1924. Scrapped, July 6, 1934
12		12			4-6-0	Jun 1881	Baldwin	5650	14x18	45"	57,000	73,700	10010	140	Rebuilt from 2-6-0, 1924. Scrapped, June 21, 1934
13		13			2-8-0	Jun 1882	Baldwin	6157	15x18	36"	51,000	57,100	12430	130	Scrapped Nov. 1927
14		18			4-6-0	Jun 1886	Baldwin	7939	16x20	51"	68,000	83,900	12370	145	Retired 1945. Boiler serv. Truckee, Scrapped 1951
15		22			4-6-0	Jun 1889	Baldwin	9929	16x20	51"	68,000	83,900	12370	145	Scrapped, Dec. 1935
16		19			4-6-0	Jun 1886	Baldwin	7941	16x20	51"	68,000	83,900	12370	145	Scrapped, Dec. 1935
17		21			4-6-0	Jun 1887	Baldwin	8487	16x20	51"	68,000	83,000	12370	145	Retired 1945. Boiler serv. Salem Ore. Scrapped 1952
			12	18	4-6-0	Dec 1911	Baldwin	37395	16x20	44"	68,000	88,900	17800	180	From NCO 1928. Donated to City of Independence 1955
			22	22	4-6-0	1899	Schenectady	5399	16x20	45"	68,000	87,150	17400	180	Originally Florence & Cripple Creek R.R., then to NCO. Purchased from NCO Sept. 1929. Scrapped 1949

This roster is as accurate as I.C.C. and other available records reveal. There is evidence that additional motive power was used on the line from 1903-1912, from a few scattered photos. These have been omitted, due to lack of confirmation.

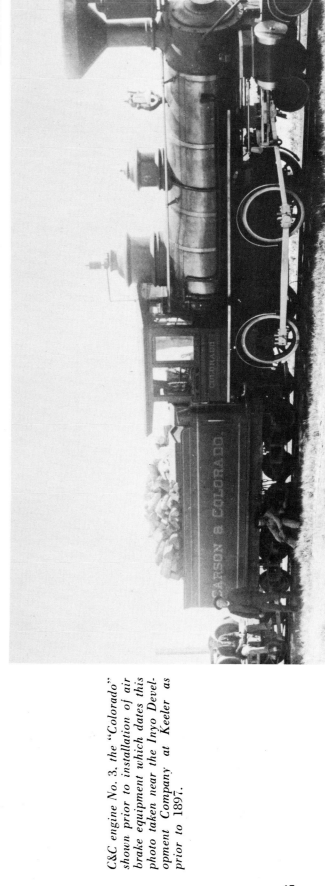

Builder's photo of engine No. 2, the "Bodie."

C&C engine No. 3, the "Colorado" shown prior to installation of air brake equipment which dates this photo taken near the Inyo Development Company at Keeler as prior to 1897.

Posing in Candelaria, Nevada in 1898 is the "Churchill," No. 4, along with Bill Robinson, Engineer; C. Meadows, Mail Clerk; Fred Barnes, Conductor; John McGillis, Fireman and Frank Regan, Brakeman.

Engine No. 6, the "Hawthorne" makes a photo stop in Keeler.

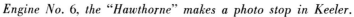

Names selected for the original C&C engines are believed to have been intended for honoring the proposed major points on the road. Three of these obviously missed this aim: the "Colorado," the "Bodie" and the "Darwin" (No. 8, shown above).

Similarity in size of the V&T "Reno" to the C&C No. 6 will allow a suitable conversion to be made. The author's model, shown below, was outshopped using commercial parts and required no machining. The tender from a Colorado & Southern was substituted for the original V&T.

49

Consolidation No. 1 is all steamed up and ready to go . . . Mina, 1931.

S.P. Narrow Gauge Locomotive No. 1

Scale: 3.5mm = 1'-0"

Copyrighted locomotive plan reprinted
drawn originally by Wayne Lincoln.

courtesy of **MODEL RAILROADER** Magazine,
Tender plan by Herb Cearley.

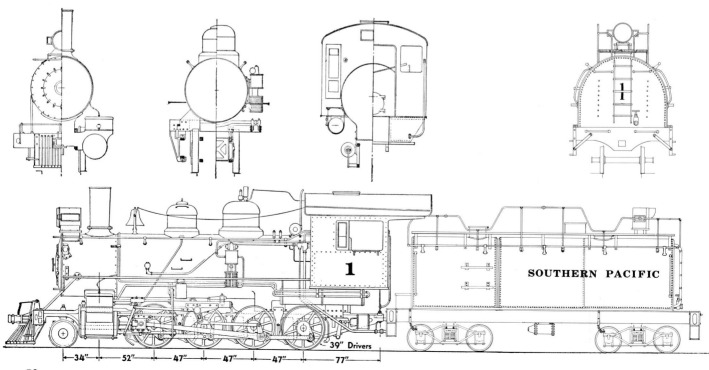

39" Drivers

34" 52" 47" 47" 47" 77"

SOUTHERN PACIFIC

1

*Now on display at Carson City, Nevada, engine No. 8 is shown
in more active days at Owenyo.*

Engine Number 9 .... Vestige of the Owens Valley

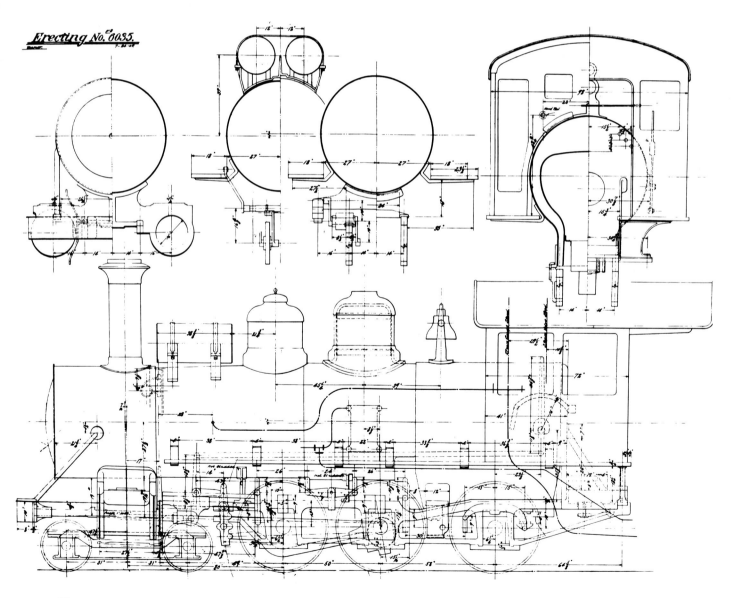

Erecting No. 6035.

GEORGE TURNER

Engine No. 9 started her career on the N.C.O. prior to being assigned to Owens Valley service in 1929. Some outward appearances have changed . . . as can be noted when comparing the original Baldwin erection drawings to the photos shown on these pages. The drawings are reproduced in ¼" scale for reference.

Tender Tank

Card No. 4247

Tank Bill No. 2677
Use 2½ Angle Iron

Tank Lugs To be used as shown
on B.L.W tracing No. 13113

Capacity:- 1800 Gals Oil
3000 Gals Water

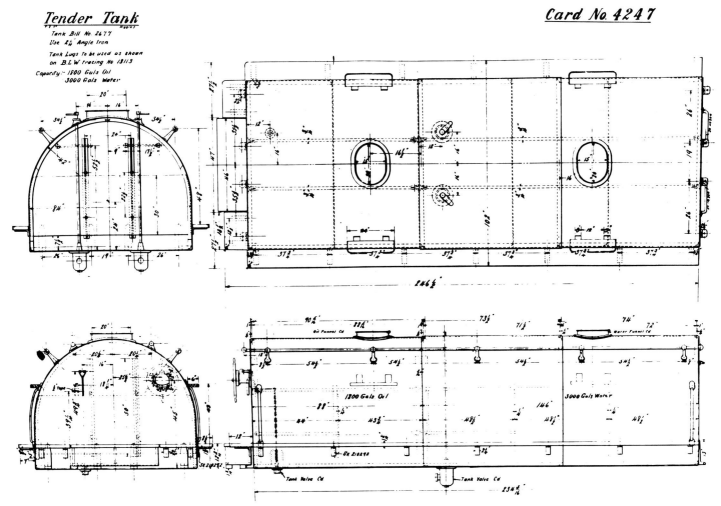

Additional views shown on this page are intended as an aid to detailing a replica of No. 9. There are over thirty parts available commercially, including Simplex tender trucks, to assist construction of an HOn3 scale engine. (Photos by the Author)

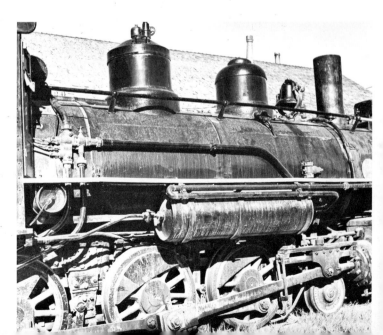

Formerly South Pacific Coast No. 17, S. P. No. 10 was used for snow removal in its last days before retiring beside the Mina engine house. One of the last original C&C engines to be scrapped, the "Benton," No. 7, awaits her fate behind No. 10.

Engine No. 14 is shown at Mina (above) and Keeler (below), during the early 30's.

ARTHUR HAIG COLLECTION

The converted (wood to oil) tender shown behind engine No. 15 was typical of those that saw original service on the South Pacific Coast and the C&C.

Engine No. 17 looks as if she were going down the street . . . without benefit of rails! This illusion resulted from a rare downpour at Keeler.

DICK DATIN COLLECTION

The only locomotive to boast of a "monkey-motion" valve gear on the S. P. narrow gauge was engine No. 18. Formerly N.C.O. No. 12, this engine has been on display at Independence, California since its retirement in 1954.

In a class by itself, engine No. 22 was the only steam locomotive assigned to the C&C-S.P. narrow gauge that wasn't built by Baldwin. The former Florence & Cripple Creek "Vindicator" was also the only piece of original Colorado motive power to see service on the Owens Valley run.

The beginning and the end of diesel power on the Southern Pacific Keeler Branch. Above: Arrival of "X1", October, 1954. Below: sporting a red and grey paint job, the "Little Giant" is shown switching at Owenyo in April of 1960, just prior to abandonment of the narrow gauge.

Modeling a western mining town will provide many hours of interesting endeavor . . . as there were no demands for "spit and polish" out West — practically anything goes! These scenes of the Colorado & California Southern on the HOn3 layout of Rollin Whittick are good examples of typical narrow gauge railroading.

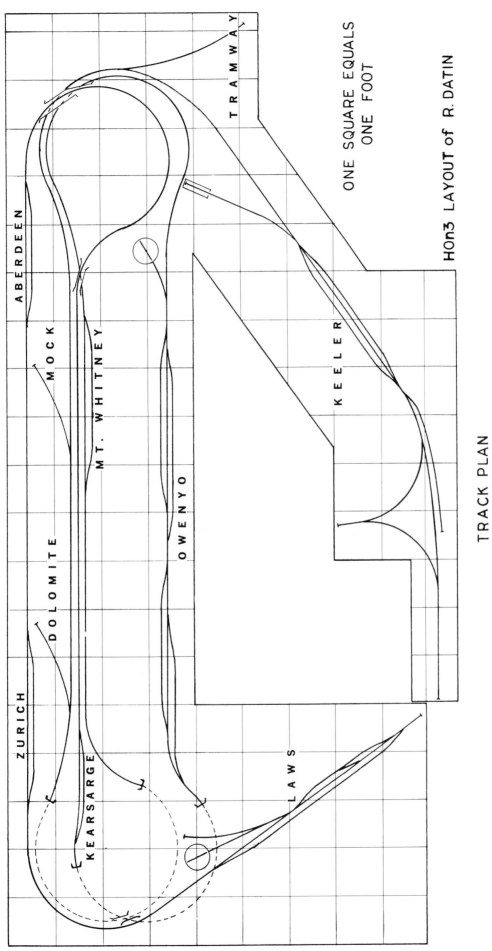

ZURICH

ABERDEEN

MOCK

DOLOMITE

MT. WHITNEY

KEARSARGE

OWENYO

TRAMWAY

KEELER

LAWS

ONE SQUARE EQUALS
ONE FOOT

HOn3 LAYOUT of R. DATIN

TRACK PLAN
KEELER BRANCH

This track layout for modeling the Keeler Branch occupies an area equal to one-half of a double garage. It provides ample trackage for extended operations, yet attains the simplicity of the point-to-point style of the prototype.

Interior showing "air conditioning" vents and coach seating accommodations.

End view of Coach No. 5, Grizzly Flats roundhouse.

Coach No. 5 prior to being sold in 1938 to (Ward Kimball) Grizzly Flats R.R. Car length: 44'-6". Car width: 8'-0".

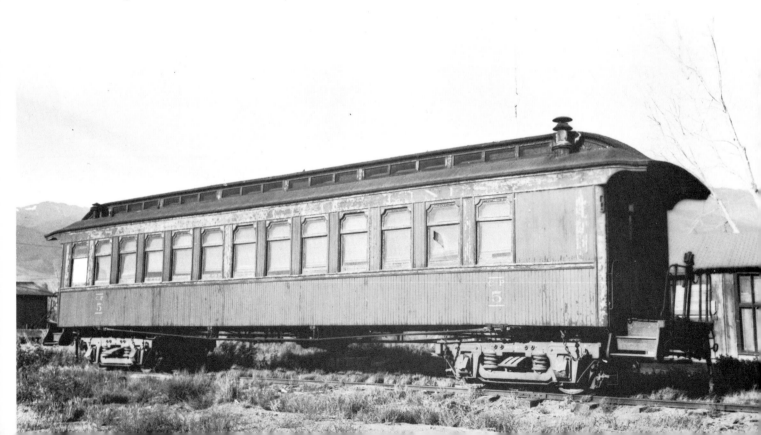

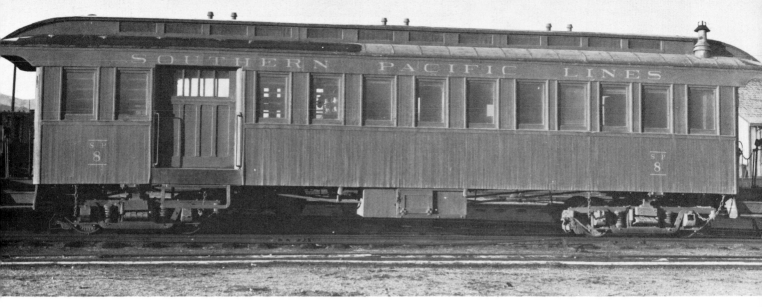

Combination car No. 8 shown at Mina in 1935 first saw service as a coach.

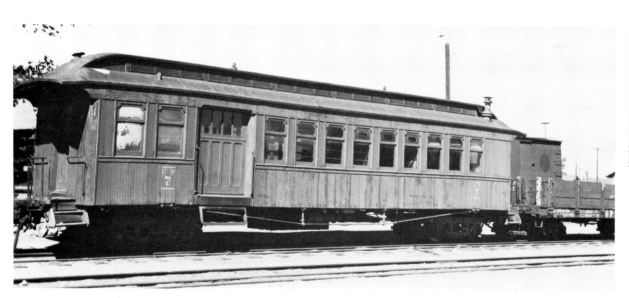

Combo No. 7 as shown here in 1937 was originally Coach No. 7. During its last days on the S.P. narrow gauge, it was lettered No. 17.

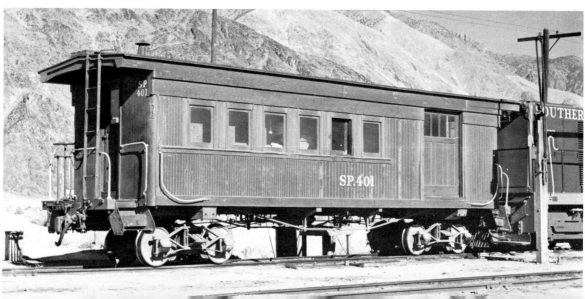

The two smallest combination cars to run on the narrow gauge were No. 400 and No. 401. (Length, 34'-3": Width, 8'-2"). Both cars were renumbered on several occasions and can best be traced by roof differences. The early photo of No. 401 was taken at Hawthorne in front of loaned Engine No. 1026 during the 1902-1905 "Boom."

Sporting freight trucks during its last days of service, No. 12 is shown at Owenyo.

Rail used for braces provided a simple answer for sagging platforms and was added prior to 1929, according to S.P. drawings.

GEORGE TURNER

GEORGE TURNER COLLECTION

ROLLIN WHITTICK

Austerity at its finest! . . . interior of No. 12.

Postal-Baggage No. 12
Drawing by: Al Barker

A familiar sight to many railfans in the last years of operations, "S.P. 12" was put to every use imaginable. Included was postal service, baggage car, caboose and even as living quarters for a period of time at Keeler. The car is now located at the Griffith Park, Calif. "Traveltown".

SCALE IN FEET AND INCHES

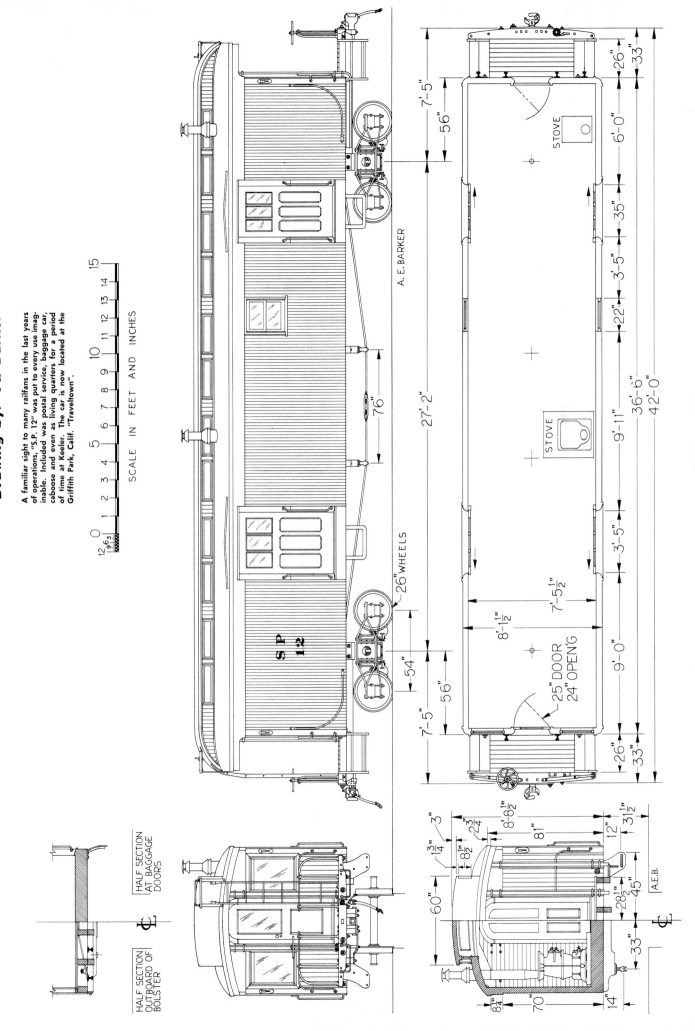

Postal baggage car No. 4 hibernates during the winter of 1936 at Mina, Nevada.

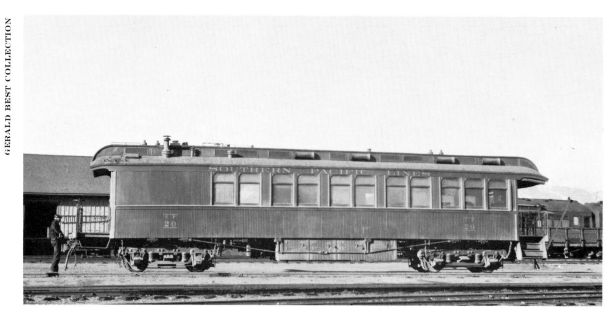

Originally built for the Florence & Cripple Creek R.R., Business car No. 20 saw service on the N.C.O. prior to assignment on the Southern Pacific as a replacement for "Esmeralda." No. 20 later became MW 5.

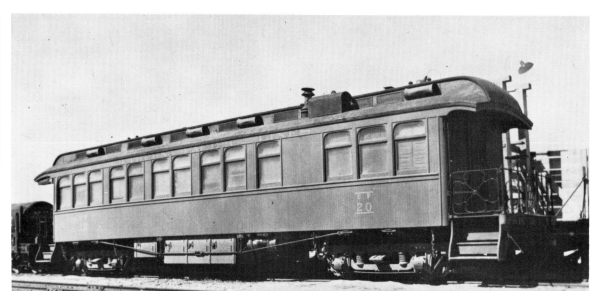

Taken in Hawthorne in 1905, this view of Esmeralda depicts the lengthened observation platform and folding step.

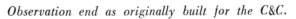

Observation end as originally built for the C&C.

. . . Business entrance.

Typical detail of all side windows.

Service entrance . . .

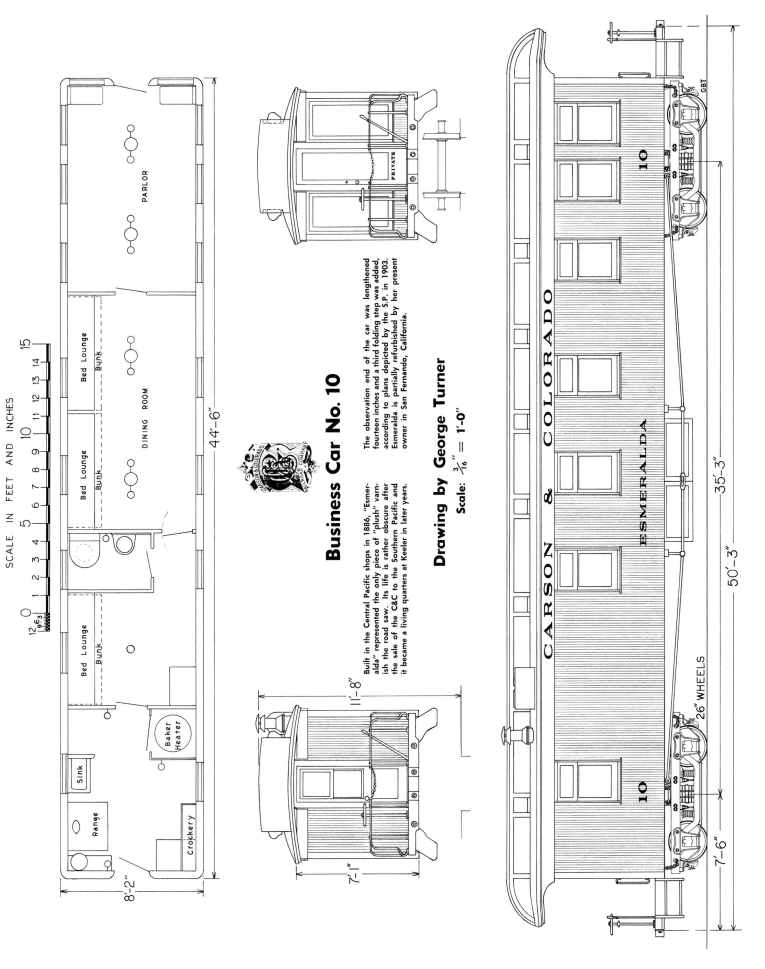

SCALE IN FEET AND INCHES

PARLOR

DINING ROOM

Bed Lounge
Bunk

Bed Lounge
Bunk

Bed Lounge
Bunk

Sink

Range

Baker
Heater

Crockery

44'-6"

8'-2"

Business Car No. 10

Built in the Central Pacific shops in 1886, "Esmeralda" represented the only piece of "plush" varnish the road saw. Its life is rather obscure after the sale of the C&C to the Southern Pacific and it became a living quarters at Keeler in later years.

The observation end of the car was lengthened fourteen inches and a third folding step was added, according to plans depicted by the S.P. in 1903. Esmeralda is partially refurbished by her present owner in San Fernando, California.

Drawing by George Turner

Scale: $\frac{3}{16}$" = 1'-0"

PRIVATE

11'-8"

7'-1"

CARSON & COLORADO

ESMERALDA

10

10

10

50'-3"

35'-3"

7'-6"

26" WHEELS

GBT

There were almost as many variations in lettering as there were differences in box cars. Most of the car alterations were traceable to the effect of extreme heat upon a particular commodity to be hauled. No explanation is available for the individuality in lettering! (Gerald Best photos)

Quite possibly these steel-sheathed C&C box cars were constructed to ward off arrows while passing through Indian country!!

No railroad is ever complete without a "Chic Sales" car!

Used for hauling a fine texture mineral called "Perlite," these converted box cars had an "A" shaped floor to assist the unloading of material out of the side doors. Loading was accomplished through the roof hatches shown, and the regular side doors were bolted shut.

GEORGE TURNER

Carson and Colorado Railroad

Ventilated Car No. 356

Several variations of this car were in evidence on the C&C. They were used extensively for perishable goods, as no refrigerator cars ever were used on the road, ironic as it seems for a desert railroad. Provisions were made to cover the louvered openings during the winter.

Drawing by Herb Cearley

Scale: $\frac{1}{4}'' = 1'\text{-}0''$

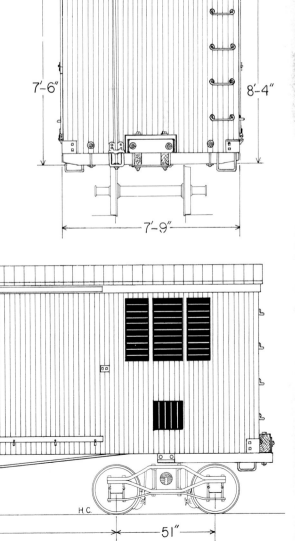

The variety of stock cars shown on this page includes a 25 ft. type (No. 153); a 33 ft. style (No. 168), and an open top 28 ft. type (No. 188, side view; No. 220, end view). Faded lettering on car No. 188 reads in part "Central Pacific," which would indicate that freight equipment at one time carried the Corporate name as did the passenger equipment.

There were hundreds of flat cars during C&C days, but the S.P. narrow gauge had only four such cars just prior to abandonment. The prime reason for this can be seen in the many types of cars built from the basic flat car, including gondolas, stock cars and MW cars.

77

In addition to the end view of the square wooden water car, domestic water car No. 61 (top left), oil tank car No. 173 (center) and auxiliary tender No. 350 are shown to illustrate the variety of tank cars used during the road's history.

Water Car No. 60

The square wooden type of tank car was representative of the Central Pacific R.R. during post-civil war years. They were used by the C&C for auxiliary tenders and also for water storage, having been built in the C.P. shops in Sacramento.

Drawing by George Turner

Scale: $\frac{1}{4}'' = 1'\text{-}0''$

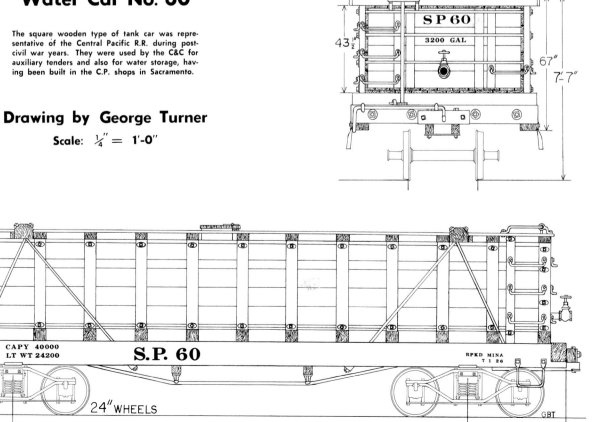

SP 60

3200 GAL

8'

43½

67"

7'-7"

CAPY 40000
LT WT 24200

S.P. 60

RPKD MINA
7 1 26

24" WHEELS

GBT

4'-3"   19'-6"   4'-3"

The 'A' frame or inverted bottom gondolas shown on these pages were built in three different lengths. The five-door style was 28 feet in length, the six-door was 33 feet long and the seven-door type was 35 feet in length . . . with the usual variations to standardization! (Photos by the author)

"A" - Frame Gondola No. 310

These cars were used for what would normally be hopper service. Material hauled in this car type was emptied out of the side doors, which were hinged at the top. Transfer trestles to reload narrow gauge ores to standard gauge cars were located at Mina, Nevada and Owenyo, California. Transfer of the loads was accomplished in "piggyback" fashion: narrow gauge on the trestle, the standard gauge cars underneath.

Drawing by Al Barker

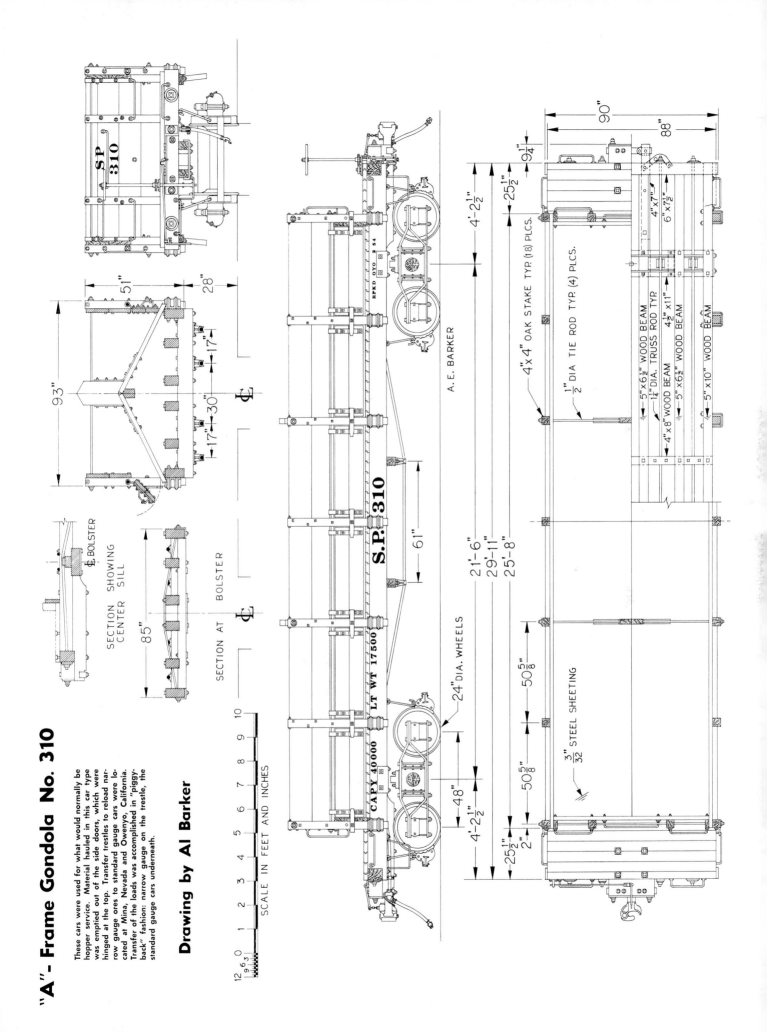

SP 310

93"

51"   28"

17"   17"   17"   30"   17"

℄

SECTION SHOWING CENTER SILL

85"

SECTION AT BOLSTER

℄ BOLSTER

℄

SCALE IN FEET AND INCHES

12 9 6 3 0   1   2   3   4   5   6   7   8   9   10

S.P. 310

LT WT 17500   CAPY 40000

RPKD OYO 2 54

61"

A. E. BARKER

24" DIA. WHEELS

48"

4'-2½"

4'-2½"

21'-6"

29'-11"

25'-8"

25½"

25½"

50⅝"   50⅝"

50⅝"

2"

25½"

3/32" STEEL SHEETING

90"

88"

9¼"

4"x7"

6"x7½"

4"x4" OAK STAKE TYP. (18) PLCS.

½" DIA. TIE ROD TYP. (4) PLCS.

5"x6½" WOOD BEAM

1¼" DIA. TRUSS ROD TYP.

4"x8" WOOD BEAM

4½"x11"

5"x6½" WOOD BEAM

5"x10" WOOD BEAM

SOUTHERN PACIFIC RAILROAD, KEELER BRANCH
Narrow Gauge Rolling Stock
January 1, 1960

LOCOMOTIVES
    #1   General Electric Diesel
    #9   Baldwin Steam, with tender

BOX CARS, 20,000 lb. cap.
    SP numbers 1, 1C, 2, 3, 4, 8, 12, 13, 14, 20, 75, 131   **12**

BOX CARS, 40,000 lb. cap.
    SP numbers 5, 6, 10, 15, 16, 17, 18, 19, 21, 23, 25, 41, 42, 43, 44, 45, 46, 47, 48, 49, 50,
        51, 52, 53, 54, 55, 56, 57, 58, 59, 61, 63, 65, 66, 67, 68, 70, 71, 77, 78, 79, 80,
        81, 82, 83, 84, 85, 86, 87, 88, 89, 90, 95, 126, 128, 129, 130, 134, 135, 136, 137,
        139   **62**

BOX CARS, 40,000 lb. cap. (Perlite "Hopper" type)
    SP numbers 9, 72, 73, 74, 76, 91, 92, 93   **8**

BAGGAGE CAR, SP #12   **1**

CABOOSE, SP #401   **1**

FLAT CAR, 20,000 lb. cap. SP #1A   **1**

FLAT CARS, 40,000 lb. cap.
    SP numbers 209, 214, 236, 259   **4**

GONDOLAS, "A" FRAME, 40,000 lb. cap. (Side door dump, inverted 'V' bottom)
    SP numbers 300, 301, 303, 304, 307, 308, 310, 311, 313, 314, 316, 317, 319, 321, 323, 327,
        328, 330, 331, 332, 333, 334, 335, 336, 337, 338, 339, 340   **28**

GONDOLAS, FLAT BOTTOM, 40,000 lb. cap.
    SP numbers 201, 202, 203, 204, 205, 206, 213, 216, 221, 222, 223, 224, 225, 226, 227, 228,
        229, 230, 232, 234   **20**

OIL TANK CAR, 3300 Gal. cap. SP #352   **1**

STOCK CARS, 20,000 lb. cap.
    SP numbers 157, 159, 162, 166   **4**

STOCK CARS, 40,000 lb. cap.
    SP numbers 160, 167, 168, 170, 171, 172, 173, 174, 176, 177, 178, 179, 180, 182, 183   **15**

WATER CAR, 3300 Gal. cap. SP #350   **1**

                                    TOTALS   **158**

Portable air conditioning for the crew is being loaded into Caboose No. 401 at Owenyo during the summer of 1949.

The Carson & Colorado - S. P. narrow gauge never included the usual caboose style in its freight equipment. No. 467 shown here (top and bottom) was rebuilt from combo No. 25 (center) and was typical of the dual purpose cars that were delegated to caboose service.

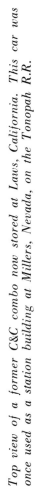

Most of the original photos of Carson & Colorado mixed trains depict one of the combination cars such as the one shown here at Mt. Montgomery.

Top view of a former C&C combo now stored at Laws, California. This car was once used as a station building at Millers, Nevada, on the Tonopah R.R.

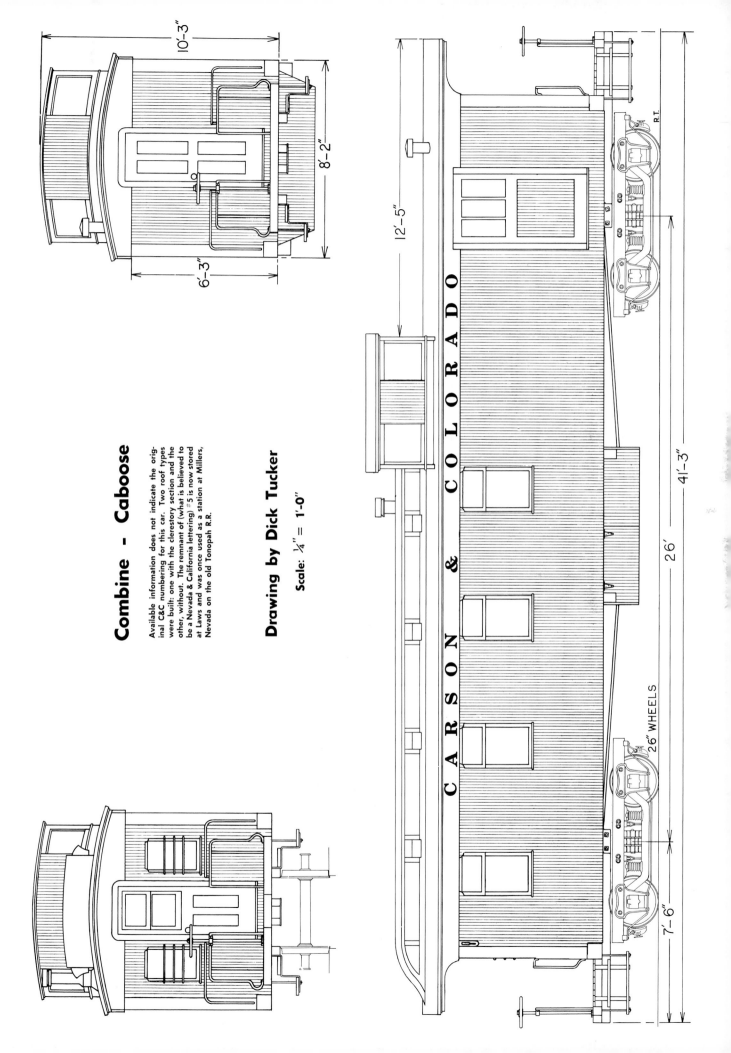

Combine - Caboose

Available information does not indicate the original C&C numbering for this car. Two roof types were built: one with the clerestory section and the other, without. The remnant of (what is believed to be a Nevada & California lettering) #5 is now stored at Laws and was once used as a station at Millers, Nevada on the old Tonopah R.R.

Drawing by Dick Tucker

Scale: ¼" = 1'-0"

10'-3"

8'-2"

6'-3"

12'-5"

41'-3"

26'

7'-6"

R.T.

26" WHEELS

C A R S O N   &   C O L O R A D O

Combination track repair - hunting expedition in Churchill canyon . . . another example of C&C railroading in a casual manner.

I've been working on the

It's a safe bet that this flagman drew a lot of attention!

*Motor car and trailer,
Laws — 1946.*

RAILROAD !

*Standard "armstrong" model
shown beside coach No. 1 in 1929,
dated back to C&C days.*

*Deluxe motor car included windshield, Model 'T' headlamp and
in the summer, an umbrella!*

Derrick car, No. 1

Wheel car, No. 1A

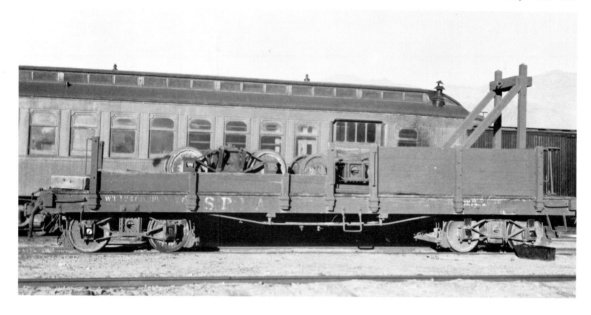

Caboose, No. 1B

Equipment car, No. 1C

When coupled together, the cars shown on these two pages made up the work train consist in 1937. Combo 1B is the same car shown on page 64 as No. 401 (*Photos, Gerald Best collection*).

Crew car, No. 1D

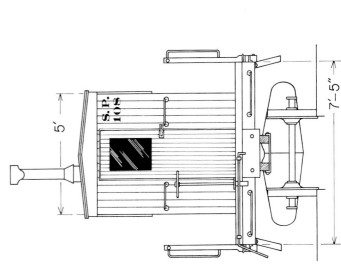

C. GRANDT COLLECTION

Flanger No. 108

This car was originally built in the Mina shops for light snow removal. Rumor has it that it was started as a project to keep the repair crews busy . . . as it never proved too good at its intended purpose! There is some evidence to bear out the story that the operator helped in the construction, as a folding "windshield" was provided on the side windows for no other apparent reason.

Drawing by Dick Tucker

Scale: ¼" = 1'-0"

82"

18'

S.P. 108

RPKD MINA
SP. 5 7 37

23'-3"

24"

10'-3"

S.P. 108

5'

7'-5"

Candelaria
Trestle

Dick Datin

Facilities,

Buildings,

and

Structures

Along the Line

*With few exceptions, the Dayton, Nevada depot set the pattern for the station build-
ings to be established along the narrow gauge.*

*The rails are gone, the water tower and engine house are down . . . yet today,
Keeler displays TWO stations! The Owenyo station was moved to Keeler in 1961
and now serves as a fire house, being located just west of the station pictured below
in 1935.*

The most impressive station on the S.P. narrow gauge was this two story structure at Mina. Built during the Tonopah "Boom," it today houses a cafe.

DONALD DUKE COLLECTION

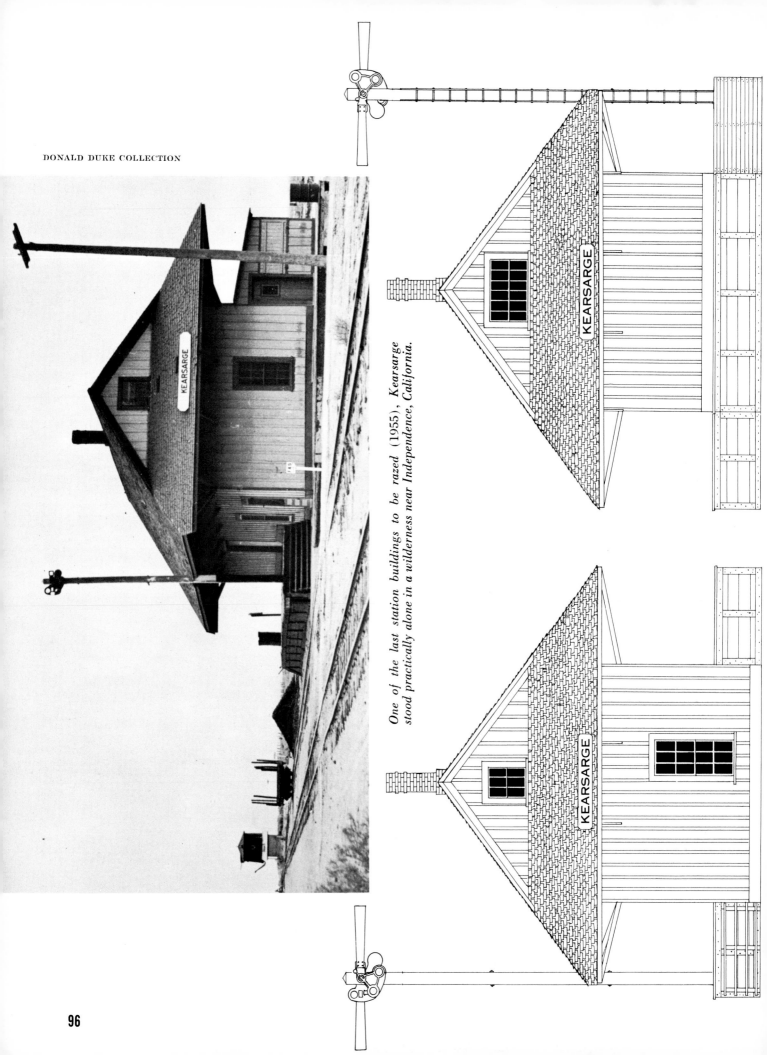

One of the last station buildings to be razed (1955), Kearsarge stood practically alone in a wilderness near Independence, California.

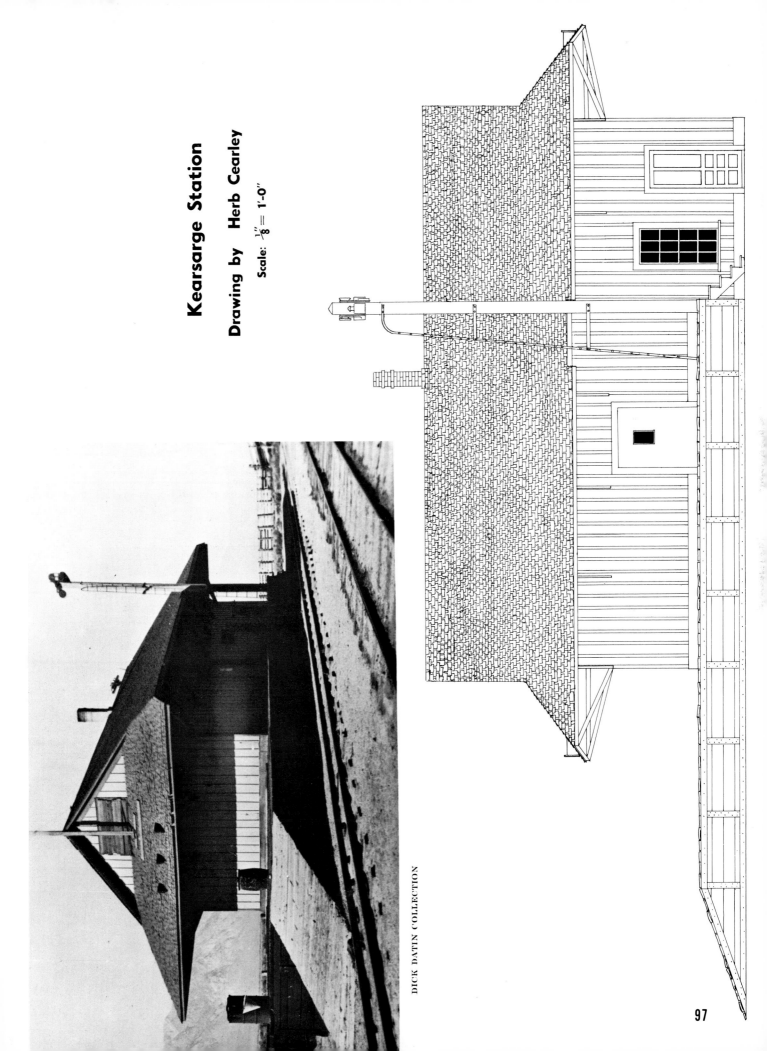

Kearsarge Station

Drawing by Herb Cearley

Scale: $\frac{1''}{8} = 1'\text{-}0''$

DICK DATIN COLLECTION

FRED HUST

Now standard gauged, Schurz, Nevada remains the headquarters for the Schurz Indian Reservation. The ghost town of Rawhide is located some 30 miles southeast. It was once planned to connect the two towns with the proposed Rawhide Western R.R., which never materialized.

Engine houses were built at Mound House, Hawthorne, Mina, Candelaria and Keeler. All except Mina were erected by the C&C and were similar to the one shown at Keeler prior to its burning down in 1946.

GEORGE TURNER COLLECTION

Dimensions for the turntables shown (Laws, above; Owenyo, below) are as follows: Bed width, 14 ft.; Bed length, 56 ft.; Center support height, from top of rail, 22 ft.; turntable support pit, 18 ft. square.

Time for a "water" break . . . Aberdeen tower, 1947.

Oil and water storage at Mina in 1910 are pictured in this early photo. The tallest water tank shown on the left is all that remains today.

GEORGE TURNER

The water and oil tanks, shown above at Laws, are now the only remaining such mementos left. The Kearsarge tank (below) was razed in 1961 and the Keeler tank was taken down and moved to Mojave, Calif. in 1962.

Mechanization was limited for the transfer of freight from the narrow gauge!

Requirements for movement of narrow gauge engines for major overhaul were handled on this transfer dock at Owenyo.

Harp switch stands such as this, shown at Zurich, were in use until World War II.

. . . riding the slim rails through the sand in days of yore, the "Slim Princess" is now no more . . .